# MIRACLES, SHOCKERS, & LONG SHOTS

# MIRACLES, SHOCKERS, LONG SHOTS

## THE GREATEST SPORTS UPSETS OF ALL TIME

BARRY WILNER & KEN RAPPOPORT

TAYLOR TRADE PUBLISHING
Lanham • New York • Boulder • Toronto • Oxford

Published by Taylor Trade Publishing
An imprint of The Rowman & Littlefield Publishing Group, Inc.
4501 Forbes Boulevard, Suite 200, Lanham, Maryland 20706

Distributed by NATIONAL BOOK NETWORK

Library of Congress Cataloging-in-Publication Data

Wilner, Barry.
    Miracles, shockers, and long shots : the greatest sports upsets of all time / Barry Wilner and Ken Rappoport.
        p.   cm.
    ISBN-13: 978-1-58979-311-8 (pbk. : alk. paper)
    ISBN-10: 1-58979-311-0 (pbk. : alk. paper)
    1. Sports upsets.   2. Sports—History.   I. Rappoport, Ken.   II. Title.
GV576.W46 2006
796.09—dc22

                                                                2006002627

∞ ™ The paper used in this publication meets the minimum requirements of American National Standard for Information Sciences—Permanence of Paper for Printed Library Materials, ANSI/NISO Z39.48-1992.

Manufactured in the United States of America.

*For Bernice, the greatest teammate a fellow could have.*
KEN RAPPOPORT


*To the Wilner clan for their unending support and love.*
BARRY WILNER

# CONTENTS

# Contents

# INTRODUCTION

Where were you when the U.S. hockey team pulled off the Miracle on Ice at Lake Placid? When Joe Namath guaranteed a victory for his lightly regarded New York Jets in the Super Bowl? When the New York Mets amazed everybody by winning the World Series over the Baltimore Orioles?

If you follow sports, you know these were some of the biggest upsets in history—and like any major historical event, will stick in our memories forever.

Ever since David knocked off Goliath, people love cheering for the underdog. When the underdog has his day, there is no more compelling drama in sports.

Starting with the U.S. victory over the Soviet Union at the Lake Placid Olympics in 1980 and ending with New England's Super Bowl victory in 2001, here are the Top 20 upsets in sports history. We have placed them in numerical order of importance, based on our own research and our combined experience of more than 50 years as sports writers with the Associated Press. Some have had international implications (the U.S. victory over the Soviets in Lake Placid), others impacted a sport (the Jets' win over the Baltimore Colts in the 1969 Super Bowl), and others blazed new trails (Texas Western's triumph over Kentucky for the 1966 NCAA basketball championship). And don't forget these stories: the greatest comeback in baseball history (the 1914 Miracle Braves), the greatest upset in horse racing history (Man o' War losing to 100-to-1 long-shot Upset in 1919), and the greatest upset in boxing history (50-to-1 underdog Buster Douglas beating Iron Mike Tyson in 1990).

Now you can relive these thrilling upsets, and others, on the following pages. And cheer for the underdog again.

# 1

## MIRACLE ON ICE

Do YOU BELIEVE IN MIRACLES?"

As the seconds ticked down, the voice of broadcaster Al Michaels resonated with excitement.

Like many others, he could hardly believe what was happening. *Miraculous* was the first word that came to his mind. Actually, the only word.

Could it be possible?

A bunch of U.S. college kids who played amateur hockey were on their way to beating the mighty Soviets—the greatest professional team in the world—at the 1980 Olympics! The same Soviet team that had whipped the National Hockey League All-Stars the year before and dominated the international hockey scene for, well, seemingly forever.

And the very same Soviet squad that had badly embarrassed the American team in an exhibition game at Madison Square Garden in New York only a week before.

What had happened since then that made such a difference?

Why were the Americans so successful in matching up with the Soviets when they got to Lake Placid?

Their story started in training camp when Herb Brooks assembled a large group of young hopefuls from all over the country.

Certainly, the American Olympic team was the best group of collegians available—some were calling it the best Olympic team in U.S. history, players who had put their NHL careers on hold to join the Olympic mission. As coach, Brooks convinced the U.S. Olympic Committee to pay the players $7,200 apiece plus expenses so he could attract the top talent in America.

But when the field of 400-odd players was finally trimmed to a few good men for the Olympics, the 20-man squad was also the youngest U.S. Olympic hockey team in history.

"People talk about our inexperience," Brooks told his team, "but we hope to use that to our advantage. We're going to rely on our intuition, on our broken-field running. The thing we have to avoid is making mistakes that will beat us."

Unlike the Europeans, whose personnel returned year after year and were essentially professional, there was no continuity on the U.S. teams.

Brooks had to shape up this eager group to match those experienced teams from other countries. Teams such as the Soviets ate, slept, and lived hockey most of the year; played in a professional league; and trained intensely.

How could Brooks possibly get his players into that kind of shape in such a short time?

The American collegians were part-time players, full-time students. Unlike the Soviets, who were part-time soldiers and full-time athletes. The only mission of the Soviet Union's team was to win gold medals in international competition. Second-place silver—and certainly third-place bronze—was not tolerated by the government. There were jokes in the Western world that a second-place finish for the Soviets meant a road trip to Siberia, or worse.

Whether it was the World Championships or the Olympics, the cocky Soviets simply had to be first. Of all the international events, though, the Olympics were the most important to the government, and the Soviets had made their mark at the Games. The USSR grabbed the gold in five of the previous six Olympics, missing only in 1960 at Squaw Valley, when the United States took its only previous Olympic hockey championship. It was quite an upset for the time, considered the biggest for Americans in Olympic history.

Now came the 1980 Games. This was years before the Iron Curtain would have a meltdown and the Soviets would be allowed to cross over to the West en masse and make their impact on the NHL. Long before names such as Mogilny, Fedorov, and Bure dotted NHL rosters, such star players were toiling only for their nation.

The 1980 team boasted a star-studded lineup that included future Hall of Fame goaltender Vladislav Tretiak, Boris Mikhailov, Alexander Maltsev, Vladimir Petrov, Vasili Vasiliev, and Valeri Kharlamov, players who had faced the NHL All-Stars in the legendary Summit Series of 1972. The Soviets also featured savvy center Igor Larionov and Slava Fetisov, one of the world's great defensemen.

But forget about them. The fresh-faced, gee-whiz American kids weren't even considered in the same class as the career-playing Czechs and Swedes.

In 1960, an underdog American team had pulled off a miracle of its own by winning the gold medal with a ragtag bunch composed of two insurance peddlers, a television ad salesman, a couple of carpenters, a fireman, and a soldier, among others.

Twenty years later, a U.S. hockey team was once more installed as a long shot in the Olympics, skating with an impossible dream.

Not that too many Americans were noticing. There were more pressing problems on their minds. American morale was very low during this depressing and tumultuous period because of American hostages in Iran, the Soviets threatening world peace by invading Afghanistan, and high inflation in the United States. With President Carter having announced a boycott of the Summer Games in Moscow, U.S.-Soviet relations had plunged dramatically. Americans needed something to pick up their spirits.

Could this spirited collection of kids do it?

If nothing else, the U.S. Olympic team had a good hockey man in Brooks. He was the last player cut from the 1960 squad and played on Olympic teams in 1964 and 1968. He coached the University of Minnesota to three national championships before taking the Olympic job.

Brooks had a rock-hard reputation. Just ask the players who danced to his whip at Minnesota. Or any of the Olympians who joined the hunt for gold and glory.

"He wouldn't let you get away with anything," said Jack O'Callahan, a defenseman on the 1980 Olympic team. "He had some players on the team that played for him at the University of Minnesota. Those guys had a love-hate relationship with him. They hated him because he was on them all the time, but they sort of really liked him because he helped make them winners."

Cold and unemotional, Brooks had a way of brutally getting right to the point. He pushed, prodded, and even insulted his players. "I wanted to do everything I could to be called an honest S.O.B.," he said.

At times, players felt Brooks was a little too honest.

Some Brooksisms:

✦ "You're playing worse every day, and right now you're playing like the middle of next month."

✦ "Gentlemen, you don't have enough talent to win on talent alone."

✦ "You're hockey players, and I don't make it a habit to pal around with hockey players."

After awhile, the American kids were joined together in a cause. The U.S. team vs. the Soviets? No, the U.S. team vs. Herb Brooks. An emotionally charged atmosphere developed: players against the coach. That type of negative reinforcement typified Brooks's coaching technique in the college ranks. Now he was using the same technique in hopes of bringing together this diverse group of strangers from different corners of America.

"You didn't have to like him," scoring star Mark Johnson said, "but you respected the stand he took and his hockey knowledge."

And under Brooks, the physical part of the game was usually far tougher than the mental. There was a terrifying drill called "Herbies"—top-speed dashes without the puck, up and down the ice for varying distances and times.

Sometimes he threatened to skate players "until they died." They believed him.

"Herbie had a way of getting his point across real quick," said forward Neal Broten.

Before the Olympics, there would be plenty of hard work. Brooks had lined up an arduous seven-month exhibition tour of 60 games with some of the toughest competition, including several professional teams and the daunting Soviets. It was dramatically different from previous years, when U.S. teams faced a lighter schedule. Under Brooks, "camp" was no vacation, but more like boot camp. Training to be a Marine seemed easier.

When the touring team was pared to 26, the U.S. Olympians had a distinctly regional flavor: Ten players that Brooks coached himself at Minnesota made the squad.

Favoritism? No, Brooks was not alone in making the selections. He brought together some of the sharpest hockey minds in the country to help him pick the team by committee. "We all agreed on 90 percent of the choices," Brooks said, defending his Minnesota selections.

Case closed.

Actually, Brooks and his staff were looking for a special kind of hockey player when they made their choices. And not necessarily the kind that would literally fight for his country. In fact, they preferred an adaptable thinking man's player willing to learn a new style of hockey.

The international style was basically foreign to the American players. Europeans skated on larger rinks, allowing for more of a free-flowing game than in North America. In seven short months, the Americans would need to adapt to this style, which featured more skill, skating, and puck handling than physical play. After all, they had to skate with the Soviets, the best-conditioned hockey players in the world. The Soviets were usually at their toughest in the third period, skating rings around their opponents with a precise, soldierlike style—as the NHL All-Stars in 1979 discovered.

Under Brooks's conditioning regimen, the American players learned about everything from anaerobics to flexibility exercises. These were tough, but not as tough as Brooks himself when it came to discipline.

Once, after the Americans skated to a desultory tie with Norway during the exhibition schedule, Brooks was enraged. He thought his players had not given their best effort. He sent

# WORLD CUP SHOCKER

Soccer was invented in England, where it has become akin to a religion.

It's an afterthought in the United States, and probably always will be, forever ranked behind football, baseball, basketball, and even auto racing in American sporting minds.

That the finest athletes in America always strayed toward any sport but soccer makes the U.S. World Cup team's achievement in 1950 absurd. Then again, absurdity is at the core of many upsets, particularly this one.

The ragtag U.S. squad, as chronicled in the recent film *The Game of Their Lives*, was made up of a few 1948 Olympians. Mostly, though, the American players were immigrants who grew up playing the game but had little top-level professional experience. Nor did they have more than a few practice sessions together before journeying to Brazil for the world championship tournament.

"I think our team was probably a little better than people gave us credit for," said Walter Bahr, one of the United States' top players. "I think a lot of us felt if we could go down there and keep the game close, we could hold our heads up."

They kept it close against Spain in their opener, leading late in the game before falling 3-1. Next up were the English, who had boycotted three previous World Cups for political reasons but were among the favorites for the 1950 championship. Led by Billy Wright, Tom Finney, and Stanley Mortensen, they were expected to overwhelm the United States at Belo Horizonte, Brazil.

"We knew we weren't in the same class as the English team," Bahr said. "But anybody worth their salt when they go out onto the field, they always think there's some possibility that something can happen, that they could steal a victory."

Stealing was pretty much what it would be. The Americans were considered among the weakest teams in the field.

England dominated the early action, coming close to scoring several times as the Americans packed in their defense, a tactic often used by extreme underdogs in soccer.

But late in the first half, Bahr took a throw-in from Ed McIlvenny and, from about 25 yards away, shot at the net. England's goalkeeper Bert Williams was lined up for a save as he moved right, but Joe Gaetjens dived, got his head on the ball, and sent it the other way for a goal.

Shockingly, the United States led.

"For us to be ahead at the half was one thing," Harry Keough said. "For us to hold it was another. I thought, 'We woke them up; shots will rain down on us now.'"

The English stormed the American net for the entire second half. Goalkeeper Frank Borghi was playing the game of his life, and the Brits became more frustrated with every save he made.

"I had quite a bit of shots," Borghi said. "I caught a lot out of the air. I had confidence in my hands."

With about 10 minutes left, Mortensen was given a free kick just outside the penalty area. Dangerous stuff.

Mortensen's lob found the head of teammate Billy Mullen, and his deflection headed toward the net. Borghi stretched and stretched—and barely tapped it away.

The English players argued the ball had crossed the goal line, but Italian referee Generoso Dattilo said no.

Deflated, the favorites lost their spirit. Then they lost the game 1-0. One of the biggest upsets the World Cup would ever see was secured, and Borghi was carried off the field by his teammates.

That was not the only low point for England. The Brits couldn't recover from the loss and fell to Spain 1-0, then went home.

To the Americans, their first-round ouster after a loss to Chile hardly mattered. The win over England provided a lifetime of memories.

"I'll never forget it," Borghi said. "But if we had played them again the next day, they'd probably beat us 10-0."


them back on the ice as punishment. They skated into the night doing the dreaded "Herbies," long after bored arena workers turned out the lights in the building.

The players were miserable, but they continued to bond as a team. Brooks was getting to them, exactly as he had wished.

"I can remember times," said Dave Silk, "when I was so mad at him I tried to skate so hard I'd collapse so I could say, 'See what you did?'"

The players were responding to Brooks's tough tactics. Playing against pro teams on the schedule only toughened them more, particularly a successful series against teams in the Central Hockey League that actually counted in the league standings.

"The character came out a little more when we played the Central Hockey League teams," Broten remembered. "They were basically all Canadian kids and I think they tried to show up the U.S. Olympic team. But we stuck together and persevered and got our systems down a little better."

The U.S. Olympians were feeling pretty good about themselves, particularly after winning a pre-Olympic tournament at Lake Placid that featured a finals win against a secondary Soviet team. "We played exceptionally well," Johnson remembered, "and it was a stepping stone to the real thing."

Then, one week before the Olympics began came a reality check for the Americans: a 10-3 drubbing by the top Soviet squad at Madison Square Garden. "We were a shaken team," O'Callahan said.

Brooks would shake them up some more.

"Right before we went to Lake Placid for the Olympics, Herb was talking about bringing in some new players from Minnesota and shaking up the team and making [captain] Mike Eruzione an assistant coach," Steve Janaszak remembered. "Well, he had a palace revolt on his hands. It was ludicrous to us."

The team threatened a wholesale walkout if Brooks went through with his announced plan. He didn't, and the 20 players who finally made up the American Olympic team were never more unified.

"That was the kind of anger Herb generated," Janaszak said.

But how would they translate that anger into winning hockey against such formidable opposition in the Olympics?

Just getting into the medal round was going to be a challenge for the Americans. Their first two opponents were none other than Czechoslovakia and Sweden, the No. 2 and No. 3 seeded teams.

Welcome to the big time, kids.

And welcome to more of Herb's histrionics.

On the first day of Olympic competition, the Americans met the Swedish team. Early in the first period, Robbie McClanahan was slammed into the boards and slumped to the ice.

His thigh pounded with pain, and he quickly signaled for a replacement. McClanahan hobbled to the locker room and took off his skates with a grimace, the sound of the crowd still ringing in his ears. Tears came to his eyes, and not only because of the pain. He had worked for seven torturous months to become a part of the Olympic team, and now it seemed his chance was over after playing less than one period at the Games.

"I can't skate on this," McClanahan complained to O'Callahan, who was not playing because of injury. "If I do, it won't be 100 percent and it's going to hurt the team."

McClanahan, a left winger on the first line, was not known as a quitter. A star for Brooks's national championship teams at Minnesota and one of the Olympic team's hardest workers, he was admired by all his teammates. But now his college days were behind. So, he thought, were his days with the Olympic team.

The period ended with Sweden ahead, 1-0. An angry Brooks pushed through the players as they piled into the locker room until finally he stood in front of the crestfallen McClanahan.

"Nobody's going belly-up," Brooks raged. "You play hurt."

McClanahan responded to Brooks's challenge—thigh injury

and all he willed himself back on the ice. And the team responded, pulling out a 2-2 tie that seemed more like a victory. With the Americans trailing 2-1 in the final minute, Billy Baker scored on a 55-footer with 27 seconds left. One point for the underdogs, another point for team unity.

"He pretty much stuck it in Herb's face," Janaszak remembered of McClanahan. "It was basically us against the coach. It was important for us collectively to help the guy out, stick together. I think this really brought the team together."

Next up: Czechoslovakia, considered the top challenger to the Soviets. The Czechs were a power in their own right, having won an Olympic silver medal in 1976 and the world championship in 1976 and 1978.

Brooks's motivational advice to his team: "You go up to the tiger, spit him in the eye and then you shoot him."

But not even Brooks could have expected the result. The Americans put on a skating clinic, spinning, circling, and weaving with masterly precision. They looked more like the Czechs than the Czechs themselves. The vaunted Czechs were caught flat-footed. The Americans rolled, 7-3.

Not that they made it easy on themselves. For the second time in two games, the Americans had fallen behind at the start. The pattern would continue for most of the Olympics. They beat Norway 5-1, Romania 7-2, and West Germany 4-2, scoring first only against Romania.

Unlikely as it seemed, the Americans made it to the medal round as one of the top four teams. Interest in the Games picked up considerably across the country. Suddenly Americans had something to take their minds off their worldly cares. The tough U.S. kids had shown plenty of grit in winning four games and tying one against some of the world's stiffest hockey competition.

But now in the medal round, the youthful Americans faced

the toughest challenge of all—the same Soviet team that had crushed them in New York only a week before the Olympics.

For the Americans, the puck stopped there. Or so everyone thought.

Despite their strong play against the other teams, few gave them a chance against the Soviets, not even the most die-hard American fans.

Brooks had a different outlook.

Shortly before sending his players out on the ice, Brooks fished a piece of paper from his pocket and read to a hushed locker room:

"You are born to be a player. You are meant to be here at this time. This is your moment."

It was the closest Brooks had ever come to praising his team on the long, arduous road to the Olympics.

*This is your moment.*

At that point, the Americans had exceeded all expectations, already playing over their heads. It was too much to ask them to reach another level. Or was it?

The Soviets scored a quick goal. For the fifth time in the Olympics, the Americans found themselves in an early hole. But back they came to tie. Minutes later, the Soviets took a 2-1 lead and appeared to be in control with the first period nearly at an end.

With five seconds remaining, Dave Christian received a pass from defenseman Ken Morrow, wound up, and took a prayer shot from mid-ice. Literally a long shot. Tretiak usually handled those as if he were picking cherries. But something unexpected happened. The great Soviet goalie failed to control the puck. Out came the rebound to Johnson, who knifed between two defensemen and scored with a second on the clock.

Just like that, the game was tied, 2-2.

"My goal gave us a lift," Johnson said. "We were supposed

to be down two, three goals and, boom, with one second left, it's tied. We're going into the locker room sky-high because the game's really close."

When the Soviets came out for the second period, the great Tretiak was sitting on the bench. The Soviets had pulled their No. 1 goalie and inserted Vladimir Myshkin in his place. Myshkin was no slouch himself, having shut out the NHL All-Stars in the 1979 Challenge Cup.

Unfazed by Johnson's goal at the end of the first period, the Soviets struck quickly in the second against Jim Craig to regain the lead, then kept up the pressure. Time and again they attacked the U.S. net, only to be turned back by Craig, now a tower of strength in goal for the Americans. Outshot 12-2 by the Soviets and generally outplayed, the Americans felt fortunate going into their locker room after two periods trailing only by 3-2. Craig had become "the Man."

*This is your moment.*

Brooks's motivational statement continued to ring in the ears of the young Americans. After all, for two periods they had given the powerful Soviets all they could handle.

Then they gave them more.

With about 12 minutes left in the third period, the Americans went on a power play. Johnson converted.

Tie score!

The crowd at the 8,000-seat Olympic Fieldhouse was on its feet, cheering and shouting, "U-S-A! U-S-A!"

Could the Americans actually hold on and tie this great Soviet team? That's what Mark Pavelich was thinking.

Not for long, though. He was too busy trying to control the puck along the boards deep in Soviet territory about a minute later. Pavelich hammered at the puck as he was smashed face-first into the glass. Somehow, the puck squirted out to the slot and onto the stick of Eruzione. The Soviets had failed to pick him up. The U.S. captain snapped a 30-foot wrist shot past Myshkin.

Bedlam!

Wire service printers rattled the score to newspapers across America: United States 4, Soviet Union 3. Editors did a double take.

But hold on! Still 10 minutes to go—an eternity in a hockey game.

"When Mike scored, it was just, 'Can we hang on, can we hang on?'" Broten remembered. "'Is Jim [Craig] really going to hold up?' I don't know if we fully believed that we could beat the Russians."

The Americans, who had taken seven months to come together, never more embraced the team concept than in the final 10 minutes against the Soviets. Covering for each other, sacrificing their bodies to block shots, weaving and circling all over the ice, and passing like pros, the U.S. kids played near-perfect hockey. They held the Soviets to only 9 shots in the final period after giving up 30 in the first two.

"Everybody had to work hard not to give them space," Craig said.

That included Craig, who was called on to make some scary game-saving stops in the closing minutes as the desperate Soviets mounted a last-gasp attack.

On the bench, Brooks was exhorting his players to "play your game . . . play your game."

He had to scream so he could be heard over the clamor in the arena. The noise volume from the excited fans went up as the seconds ticked down. In the ABC broadcast booth, Michaels had to keep calm. He was trying to figure out what to say if the Americans managed to hold on. "I remember thinking of one word in my mind—*miraculous*."

Miraculous, it was.

*Team USA celebrates after stunning the Soviets 4-3 at the 1980 Olympics.*

"Five seconds left in the game . . ."

Then four, three, two, one, and the puck skittered out to center ice.

"DO YOU BELIEVE IN MIRACLES?" an exuberant Michaels shouted over the tumult in the arena.

Then he answered his own question.

"YES!"

With the sound of the game-ending buzzer signaling a 4-3 U.S. victory, the stadium erupted. The building shook as if in the middle of an earthquake.

The American players jumped over the boards and pressed together in spasms of joy, their sticks raised high in victory. Some players tossed their sticks into the stands. Craig, an American flag draped over him, searched for his dad—his words to a teammate ("Where's my father?") easy to lip-read on TV. As the euphoric Americans hugged each other, their faces gleaming with sweat and wreathed in smiles, the grim Soviets watched the celebration in shock.

A nation celebrated, too. People danced in the streets.

WE BEAT THE SOVIETS!

They pounded on their horns while driving.

WE BEAT THE SOVIETS!

They cried in disbelief.

WE BEAT THE SOVIETS!

It was more than a great upset, more than a game. It was a symbol for Americans: good triumphing over evil, and a country triumphing over its own demons. Americans hadn't had a reason to feel patriotic as a country for a long time, and this victory against their vastly superior opponent gave them that reason. It was one of those rare times a sporting event provoked a national emotion.

The hostage situation in Iran. The Soviet Union's threat to world peace in Afghanistan. America's economic problems at home. All these faded for Americans in the glow of the Olympic victory. The college kids had shown them, actually reinforced what they already knew about the American way: Hard work, self-confidence, and self-sacrifice can surmount any obstacle, no matter how great.

In an almost anticlimactic final in which they once again needed to rally, the Americans beat Finland 4-2 for the gold medal.

A nation had its self-esteem back.

# 2

## THE GUARANTEE

When the Baltimore Colts should have been celebrating, they were seething.

The Colts had just demolished the Cleveland Browns 34-0 to win the 1968 NFL championship. They were being hailed as one of the great teams in pro football history after going 13-1 and scoring a phenomenal 402 points while allowing 144.

Their victory over Cleveland meant the Colts would represent the NFL in something that now was being billed as the Super Bowl. Called the AFL-NFL Championship Game in the two previous installments, there was little that was super about the matchups. The Green Bay Packers romped over Kansas City and then Oakland, securing the established NFL's reputation as the premier league in the pro game.

And now the upstart AFL was sending the New York Jets, a finesse team led by a playboy quarterback, as its sacrificial lamb to the mighty Colts. The Jets were considered inferior to the 1966 Chiefs and 1967 Raiders, so what chance did they have against a Baltimore roster regarded more highly than Green Bay's champions?

The Jets believed they had a great chance to win because they were loose, relaxed—and predicting victory.

"We were watching films of the Colts after the point spread had been announced," tight end Pete Lammons said. "After seeing some of the things they did, I got up and said to everybody, 'If we watch this anymore we're going to get overconfident.'"

Added Joe Namath, the image-conscious quarterback—you know, the furs, the pantyhose commercial, the Broadway Joe image—who would lead the heavy underdogs into the Orange Bowl:

"When we saw the point spreads, that we were 17 and 17½-point and 18-point underdogs, we just laughed. And after we watched film of the Colts, we laughed even more. We were convinced we were going to win."

The oddsmakers obviously weren't. Nor was the public, which began betting so heavily on Baltimore that the line reached unparalleled numbers in championship game history. The fans looked at the Jets' close win over the Raiders in the title game—a victory secured, in part, because of critical mistakes by Oakland—and were convinced this was a mismatch of majestic proportions.

"I thought it was going to be a runaway because the Colts were considered one of the great NFL teams and I didn't think the Jets were anywhere near our best," Kansas City Chiefs owner Lamar Hunt said.

Green Bay was favored by 14 points against the Chiefs, by 15 against the Raiders, and because the Packers won easily, it seemed natural that the spread would be higher for the Colts-Jets. Indeed, some bettors were willing to give as many as 20 points.

Some NFL people did. There were rumors for years, in fact, that Colts owner Carroll Rosenbloom was a heavy bettor and that he laid the 20 for the game.

Most pro players claim they aren't aware of such outside shenanigans, but they are. Sure, they attempt to keep the distractions to a minimum and not allow them to infiltrate the "inner circle" all athletes try to form.

The Jets were very cognizant of how they were being downgraded, even scorned.

"There were a lot of guys who wanted to get even with the NFL," said Jets receiver Don Maynard, who became an AFL star after beginning his career with the New York Giants in the late 1950s. "I don't cuss very often, but I'd say you're damn right we wanted to prove ourselves. I was so sick of that garbage about us not being good enough."

But the Colts were sick of what they were hearing from the other side. Where was the respect?

Almost from the moment they knew the Jets awaited them on January 12 in the Super Bowl, Colts players were livid that the Jets considered themselves equals. Even superior.

"We had the wrong attitude," said Colts tight end John Mackey, who would go on to make the Pro Football Hall of Fame. "We started to believe we were this prohibitive favorite, that all the Baltimore Colts had to do was show up and collect the trophy. We announced our victory party plans on the Wednesday before the game. We even cut up the winners' shares at the pre-game meeting. Can you believe that?"

Well, yes.

Anyone who closely examined the results of the 1968 season might have felt the same way. Had they dug deeper, though, perhaps certain elements of the AFL's and NFL's makeup at the time would have yielded some clues that the Jets might not be overwhelmed from the opening kickoff.

For one, while the NFL clearly deserved the favorite's role, the overall skill level in the league was not much higher than in the AFL. NFL defenses tended to be stingier, in part because the AFL had embraced some of the "outlaw" attitude of Raiders owner Al Davis. The AFL had star quarterbacks galore, and Namath probably wasn't the best of them at the time. Not with Len Dawson and John Hadl and Daryle Lamonica also around.

Indeed, AFL teams were capable of shootouts every week, another reason NFL purists scoffed at "the new league." They preferred the man-eating defenses, the Monsters of the Midway and Fearsome Foursomes, to the run-and-gun philosophy of the AFL.

But that style made AFL players and teams more adaptable. No matter how good the defenses they faced, the AFL offenses, including Namath and the Jets, were capable of adjusting their schemes and play-calling. They had so much in their arsenals, and most opponents could not prepare for everything.

The AFL also had benefited from increasing success in the draft. Personnel men around the league had established strong scouting systems, and they sometimes shared information during the "football war" days of the early and mid-1960s. Back then, it was just as important to land marquee college players and potential future stars for the league as for a specific team.

Call it collusion, if you like, but that strategy not only helped the AFL further establish its credentials but also impressively enhanced the talent base. And it kept the likes of a Namath or Fred Biletnikoff or Lance Alworth—all future Hall of Famers—out of the NFL.

The Colts didn't recognize how far the AFL and its champion had come. What Mackey and Mike Curtis, Earl Morrall and Johnny Unitas, Bubba Smith and Ordell Braase, Jimmy Orr and Tom Matte saw was image, not substance.

To an extent, the Jets even encouraged that approach.

"We were the chosen team of the AFL," star defensive end Verlon Biggs said. "We changed the look of pro football with the long hair and the white shoes. We were the Beatles of pro football."

And that ticked off the establishment no end.

"To say that there was a friendly relationship between the owners of the two leagues would be misleading," said Cleveland Browns owner Art Modell, who, coincidentally, would move his team into the AFC from the NFC to solidify the merger in 1970.

"We wanted to beat the AFL into the ground, and we all believed the Colts would do just that to the Jets."

A confrontation between Namath and hard-nosed Colts defensive lineman and kicker Lou Michaels magnified those feelings. Both were in a bar during Super Bowl week when someone attempted to introduce them.

"Namath didn't shake hands or say hello," Michaels said. "He just said, 'We're going to kick the bleep out of you and I'm the guy who's going to do it.' I said, 'I'd like to have you outside for one minute,' and he said, 'I'm not a dummy, I won't do that.'"

Now, Namath *was* no dummy. And no, Namath wouldn't go outside with Michaels. Indeed, he wound up picking up the tab at the bar for Michaels and other companions, then drove Michaels back to his hotel.

There was something else outlandish Namath would do.

He attended a dinner at the Miami Touchdown Club. Such things often are nonevents, with club members mingling with big stars, getting autographs, chatting, even making business offers.

Broadway Joe turned this into an event, however. He also turned the rest of the week, and the game itself, into a monster. Indeed, it could be argued that the American holiday that now is Super Bowl Sunday was created when Namath opened his mouth at that dinner and said:

"They've been talking all week. Now it's my turn. I've got news for you. We're going to win. I guarantee it."

Namath had not only violated every athletic credo outside of boxing and wrestling—always praise your opponents, never give them any bulletin-board fodder—but had also disobeyed coach Weeb Ewbank.

Ewbank, knowing Namath's penchant for the outrageous, had ordered his quarterback to watch what he said, to play it straight.

And Ewbank knew what he has doing. During his stint as an NFL coach, he led the Colts to two championships. He also recognized that the Colts might be somewhat cocky, and he didn't want any of his players—particularly Namath—to rile them up.

After the guarantee, the Colts were feverish in their desire to pummel Joe and the Jets.

"Weeb was upset. Boy, he was upset," Namath recalled. "He'd looked at the films, too, and he saw that they were beatable, that we'd seen everything they could challenge us with during the season from teams like Oakland and Buffalo and Houston.

"He didn't want to give them any fuel to get fired up, so when I [guaranteed a victory], he was angry. He had a right to be."

Still, when Ewbank was asked about Namath's comments, he replied, "It ain't often that my quarterback whistles Dixie."

While Namath was being scorned in many quarters for his cockiness, egotism, even arrogance, he also was praised by others who saw through the bluster.

"He had nothing to lose doing that," said Sonny Jurgensen, another Hall of Fame quarterback with few inhibitions. "He believed it and that was good. It was motivating for him and the team. It had psychological impact."

Perhaps that was all it was intended to do. Namath certainly wasn't about to retract his comments. He didn't need to embellish them, either.

And playing in New York, he understood the attention anything controversial he said or did would attract.

"I didn't think I put any extra pressure on myself," he said. "Pressure is what you make it. Those comments didn't put any extra on me. It was like going into most big games, kill or be killed. You need to do it. The pressure came from the fear of losing.

"For two weeks, we were told how we were going to lose. When you keep hearing your team isn't going to win, you get angry and frustrated. The anger festers. Anger is a good thing to have.

"I never guaranteed any game prior to that," Namath added. "I don't know if it was just a guardian angel. It was basically anger with the way we thought knowledgeable people were painting us."

One of the men who would paint word pictures of the contest, NBC's Curt Gowdy, had an obvious interest in seeing a close game. It would not only boost ratings but also attract favorable attention to his network broadcast.

In light of that tie-in, Gowdy's opinion might have been considered clouded, not prescient, after he attended a Jets workout during Super Bowl week.

"It was the weirdest practice," Gowdy said. "I was there for an hour and a half and there wasn't a word spoken. All you could hear was the thud of body hitting body, nobody said anything.

"They were the most maligned, insulted boys in the country. They were pissed. They were determined."

And they were 17-point underdogs. Or 18. Or 20.

With 75,377 fans at the Orange Bowl and tickets being scalped for as much as $100—big bucks in 1969—the Jets looked relaxed during pregame drills. The Colts appeared uptight, just as Namath and Ewbank hoped.

After astronauts James Lovell, Frank Borman, and William Anders recited the Pledge of Allegiance and all the pregame hoopla was hooped out, the Jets, in white and green, and the Colts, in blue with the famed horseshoe on their helmets, kicked off the game that would change pro football forever.

Not much happened in the first 10 minutes as both sides, like cautious boxers, felt out the opponent. For the Jets, that was a good thing: What heavy underdog is supposed to be tied 0-0 at any point beyond the opening moments of a big game?

Near the end of the first quarter, however, the Colts recovered a fumble by Jets receiver George Sauer—who only had the best hands on the entire team. Baltimore was set up at the New York 12, and it would be only a few minutes, even seconds, before the Colts were ahead to stay, right?

Uh, no. Not on this day.

Morrall, whose work in replacing the injured Unitas earned the veteran the league's most valuable player award, passed to Tom Mitchell in the end zone. The ball, which was on target, should have resulted in a touchdown.

Instead, it ricocheted off Mitchell's shoulder pad to Jets cornerback Randy Beverly.

"That showed where things were going," said cornerback Johnny Sample, who played for the Colts in the NFL before rejoining Ewbank with the Jets in the AFL. "If plays had to be made, we were going to make them."

They began making them on the ground. While Namath's arm was the crown jewel of the offense, the true centerpiece was the versatile running game of fullback Matt Snell and halfback Emerson Boozer. Snell was the power man, but he also was the main runner, which was not unusual in the 1960s. Boozer was the shifty, speedy outside threat and a premier receiver out of the backfield.

From watching film—no, Namath was not out partying all the time—the quarterback sensed that his quick yet powerful offensive line of guards Dave Herman and Randy Rasmussen, tackles Sam Walton and Winston Hill, and center John Schmitt could dominate the trenches. Yes, they were facing the likes of Smith, Braase, and Michaels. Yes, they were going up against a team that had refined blitzing, something coach Don Shula called "what got us here."

But Namath and Ewbank were determined to offset Baltimore's defensive strengths by using the Jets' own strengths.

Inexorably, they marched downfield from their 20. Snell, who would finish the game with 121 yards on 30 carries—he probably deserved MVP honors over Namath—gained 26 yards on four straight carries.

Then the Jets went to the air just when the Colts had become accustomed to dealing with the run. Namath found Sauer for 14 yards, then 13.

Sauer would be Namath's main aerial weapon all game because Maynard had tweaked his leg and was going only half speed. But the lack of production from the future Hall of Famer (no receptions) didn't slow the Jets as Sauer came through with eight catches for 133 yards.

As New York approached the Colts' goal line, viewers throughout America were stunned to see Baltimore reeling. But not as stunned as the Colts themselves.

"It was frustrating because of how they were mixing it up, using power runs and then passing," Smith said. "They had a good game plan and they were taking it to us at that point."

From the Baltimore 4, Namath knew exactly what play he wanted.

"That touchdown started happening before the ball was

*Joe Namath watches the Jets defense stop Baltimore*
*during the 1969 Super Bowl.*

snapped," Namath said. "I saw them send a defensive player on the field and knew what formation they would be in. We didn't even take three-point stances. I believed that first split second put us in the end zone."

And put the Jets ahead 7-0 as Snell swept left for the TD.

To their credit, the Colts responded with a strong drive, but they missed a field goal. So did the Jets. And after Tom Matte burst through the line for a 58-yard run, the longest play of the day, the Colts were in scoring range again.

Then Morrall, looking more like a journeyman than an MVP, made another mistake. He tipped off his pass to Willie Richardson, and Sample cut in front of the receiver to pick it off.

"I had studied the films all week and knew Richardson had a tendency to try to get on the inside of me," Sample said. "I just closed down and made the interception. It was really a pretty easy play. I read it right away."

Such turnovers were uncharacteristic for Baltimore. But the Colts also were resilient, and they moved into Jets territory late in the half. That set up the most critical play of the biggest upset in pro football history.

Shula, a straitlaced coach not known whatsoever for trickery, called for a flea-flicker. Morrall handed the ball to Matte, who faked running toward the line to draw in the linebackers and secondary. Then Matte pitched the ball back to the quarterback.

Morrall scanned the field. The Jets had allowed Orr to sneak free deep, perhaps 15 yards behind any defenders. They had been suckered.

But Morrall didn't see Orr. His body was turned just enough that his main focus was on Jerry Hill, the fullback who had gone down the middle of the field. Morrall put some air under his pass, a huge error, and his lob was intercepted by safety Jim Hudson.

"If I had rifled it, we would have had a touchdown," Morrall claimed.

"I was waving that I was free, but Earl couldn't see me," bemoaned Orr. "It was a big play."

A big letdown for Baltimore, as well. The Jets led 7-0 at halftime.

In the locker room, Ewbank and his coaches emphasized

the need to simply continue what the Jets were doing. No need to get fancy; the game plan was working.

The other locker room was a frantic scene. Shula was livid about the mistakes, telling his team, "This is not the way we play football."

Shula would go on to become the winningest coach in NFL history and capture two straight Super Bowl crowns with Miami. His 1972 Dolphins would be the only undefeated team in league history. But he couldn't get his message across to this group. Maybe the Colts believed everything they heard and read about themselves. Maybe the accolades about being one of the greatest teams in pro sports history turned their resolve into Jell-O.

On the first play after the second-half kickoff, the sure-handed Matte fumbled. Not exactly what Shula and the Colts had in mind.

Jim Turner made a 32-yard field goal off the turnover for a 10-0 lead. It became 13-0 when Turner kicked a 30-yarder later in the period.

That hardly is an insurmountable lead, but the way Baltimore was performing, the Jets could have begun engraving championship rings.

Down by 13 points, Shula turned to Unitas, a move the coach never expected to make. Morrall had been so steady and so much in command throughout the season and the playoffs that Shula couldn't imagine a scenario in which the Jets would force him to bring on Johnny U.

Unitas, who quarterbacked Ewbank's Colts to NFL crowns in 1958—in the first overtime game in league history—and 1959, had been sidelined with a sore arm. But he was needed now.

"I felt fine," he said. "I didn't have as much velocity as I'd like to have, but if I'd been given the whole half to work, I think we could have turned the thing around."

The Jets were more concerned with Unitas in the game than they were against Morrall. But not much more concerned.

"Johnny was one of the smartest quarterbacks ever," said linebacker Larry Grantham. "But there wasn't much he could do at that point but throw. They were behind and they needed points right away."

They couldn't get them, though. Just after Namath led another clock-eating drive to Turner's third field goal, Unitas was intercepted by Beverly, New York's fourth pick of the game.

It was at this juncture of the game that Namath took charge on the sideline. He told his teammates not to let down with victory so close. Don't get cocky, don't taunt the Colts.

"We needed to act like champions if we were going to be champions," he said.

First, they had to get through the fourth quarter, and when Unitas finally got the Colts going, taking them 80 yards to Hill's 1-yard TD run, there were a few sweaty palms in white and green.

Then Baltimore recovered an onside kick. Uh-oh.

Unitas took the field down 16-7, fully expecting to pull his team within 2 points. Grantham, the leader of the Jets defense, had other thoughts.

"We weren't backing down," he said. "We weren't going to get beaten with a big play, but we also weren't going to let Unitas pick us apart."

With controlled aggression, if you will, the Jets made the Colts use up precious time moving downfield through the rapidly settling darkness. When Baltimore reached the New York 19, the Jets stiffened. Unitas's fourth-down pass was batted away by Grantham with 2:21 on the clock.

At that moment, Namath turned to Ewbank, gave him a wink, and headed onto the field to finish it off.

Although the Colts did get the ball back once more, in the

dying seconds, the verdict already had been reached. Jets 16, Colts 7.

AFL rejoicing, NFL in disgrace.

"Down in the [Jets'] locker room, there was virtually an AFL owners meeting," said Hunt, the guiding force among AFL owners. "There was a great feeling of euphoria and accomplishment. I never felt that way about another team winning before."

Modell, meanwhile, felt like his NFL cohorts. Where could they go to hide?

"They stuck it to us pretty good," Modell said. "There was a scheduled postgame party at Carroll Rosenbloom's house and it wasn't a party, it was more like a funeral. It was not one of our better days."

In truth, it was a great day for pro football. The Jets' victory helped relieve a stalemate in negotiations over the AFL-NFL merger. NFL owners wanted the 26 teams split the way they were situated before the merger: 16 in the NFL, 10 in the AFL.

NFL commissioner Pete Rozelle preferred a 13-13 split, but he was of no mind to take on his owners if their league kept dominating the title game. When it was the Jets—the AFL's Jets—who did the dominating, the 13-13 alignment was given life.

"We thought the NFL was superior, but history has proved our judgment wrong," Modell declared.

"The game definitely helped that along," said Hunt, noting that the Browns, Colts, and Steelers now had more incentive for a switch of leagues. "A person like an Art Modell, who had a great team with a great history, could justify the move to the AFC because the Browns would be playing Joe Namath and the Jets."

So the legacy of Super Bowl III was a revamped, balanced NFL that would soon become America's pastime, which it remains today.

But the lasting image of the game is Namath trotting off the field, his index finger held high above his head.

"That is so special to me, I don't know if anyone could understand it," Namath said years later. "It was the most tingly feeling inside of me. Waving the finger wasn't really my style. I just appreciated being able to win that game. You could see my head's down as if to say, 'I humbly accept the title.'"

# 3

## THE MIRACLE BRAVES

One miracle in a season should be enough for most baseball teams. Could the Boston Braves make it two in 1914?

They had already pulled a pennant out of a hat, you could say. Now they were hoping to make the Philadelphia Athletics disappear in the World Series.

Connie Mack's princely players were gunning for their fourth world title in five seasons. They had already won four American League pennants in that period. They were huge favorites to win the Series. Many sports writers were predicting a sweep.

The Braves? Sure, they had staged an incredible comeback in the second half of the season to snatch the National League pennant away from the favored New York Giants, who had won three straight flags.

But what chance did they have in the World Series against a Philadelphia team featuring five future Hall of Famers, the famous $100,000 Infield, and a formidable pitching staff that looked like a million?

Not only were the A's considered far superior to the Braves, but the American League also was viewed as a stronger league than the National in overall talent. The AL had won the previous four World Series.

That the Braves were playing in a World Series at all was somewhat of a miracle. In 1913, they finished in fifth place with a 69-82 record in George Stallings's first year as manager. And that was their highest finish in 11 years!

The second-division finish continued a sorry history for the Braves.

In 14 seasons from 1900, the generally accepted advent of the modern game, the Braves could boast of only one winning year. From 1909–1912, the heart of the "dead ball era," the Braves averaged 104 losses a season. Needless to say, they finished last each of the four years.

Enter Stallings, son of a Confederate war hero, who had dropped out of medical school to play professional baseball. He did play in the majors, but not much, with a career batting average of .100 in seven games as a catcher.

He had more success as a manager, leading Detroit into third place in 1901 in the American League's first year. He also had brief managerial stints with the Philadelphia Phillies in the National League and New York (before becoming the Yankees) in the American.

Stallings also managed in the minors and developed a reputation for his wildly superstitious nature. According to one story, a player walked up to Stallings before a game and said, "George, we're going to win today."

Stallings asked the player how he could be so certain. The player replied: "I saw a load of barrels go by."

The team won, and Stallings added another superstition to

his list, hiring a man to drive barrels around the ballpark before games.

"All ballplayers are superstitious, but I still think my father was the champ," said George Stallings Jr. in a 1964 interview.

Stallings's son remembered that his father carried around a rabbit's foot for good luck.

"All the hair had been rubbed off from wishing and the hide had the brilliance of a bald head. When things were going badly . . . Dad would rub that rabbit's foot until it limped."

Stallings's personality might be described as schizo-phrenic—he was cultured and refined off the field and a pro-fane and testy tyrant in the dugout.

In either case, the native of Augusta, Georgia, looked the part of a southern gentleman with his smart wardrobe. Stall-ings usually sported a three-piece suit, bow tie, and straw hat.

"He was a great manager," said Charles (Chuck) Deal, who played the lion's share at third base for the Braves in 1914 after regular Red Smith was hurt.

Remembering Stallings in an interview with *Baseball Digest* in 1964, Deal said, "He used to slide up and down that bench, suffering on every play. One minute he'd be praying and the next minute he would be cursing. How that man could curse! But he was a grand man!"

When he wasn't cursing, Stallings could be inspirational. His favorite slogan to the Braves: "You can win! You must win! You will win!"

But winning didn't come all that easy in his first season at Boston's helm. In 1913, Stallings used a total of 46 players try-ing to find the right mix.

Things didn't look any more promising in 1914.

When Stallings assembled the Braves that spring, there were a lot of uncertainties. The outfield was far from set. The pitch-ing didn't look all that terrific, either.

Considering that the Braves were not an especially good hitting team, they had to rely heavily on pitching to win games. This area looked like headache number one to Stallings. George "Lefty" Tyler was the most experienced on the Braves' staff, but in three years of big-league ball had put together a mediocre 35-49 record. His 22 losses in 1912 topped the National League.

Dick Rudolph at 14-14 and Bill James at 6-10 were no more impressive. And this trio made up the "big three" of the Boston staff. The rest was a combination of rookies and veterans with losing records.

One part of the team that didn't figure to give Stallings too many headaches was the middle infield.

During the winter the Braves picked up second baseman Johnny Evers, a onetime legend in Chicago who had fallen out of favor with the Cubs.

A player-manager in Chicago, Evers was dumped as manager after the team finished third. He threatened to jump to the newly formed Federal League but wound up with Boston in a trade. A $25,000 bonus from the Braves, huge for the time, helped change Evers's mind about joining the new outlaw league. In addition, Evers was the Braves' highest paid player at $7,500, according to Deal.

Evers had played on four pennant winners and on two World Series champions and provided veteran leadership and a cocky, hard-nosed attitude. He was chosen the Braves' captain and immediately became Stallings's alter ego on the field. Evers, a perfectionist like Stallings, drove his teammates unmercifully. Woe to the player who failed to hustle every minute of every game and every practice.

"Johnny Evers was our tough guy," Deal said. "He was a crafty little bugger. He used to give the umpires heck about everything. It got so as they'd walk him just to get rid of him. They'd never call a strike on him, just wave him to first."

In Chicago, Evers was part of a celebrated double play combination with shortstop Joe Tinker. Along with first baseman Frank Chance, the three were immortalized by New York newspaper columnist Franklin Pierce Adams in a poem titled "Baseball's Sad Lexicon."

Expressing his dismay at the continued success the Cubs and their celebrated infield had against his beloved Giants in 1910, Adams wrote:

> These are the saddest of possible words:
> Tinker to Evers to Chance.
> Trio of bear cubs and fleeter than birds,
> Tinker and Evers and Chance.
> Ruthlessly pricking our gonfalon bubble,
> Making a Giant hit into a double—
> Words that are heavy with nothing but trouble,
> Tinker to Evers to Chance.

Now in Boston, Evers would team with Walter "Rabbit" Maranville, a colorful and crafty shortstop who was the favorite of fans and media alike.

The pixielike Maranville was known for his "vest pocket" catches, snaring pop flies with his hands cupped at the belt buckle. Also for jumping into hotel fish ponds and into the arms of beefy teammates, his cap comically pulled down sideways over one ear.

"Maranville was our clown," Deal said. "Rabbit was all fun. He'd go anywhere and do anything. He used to take this great big old bulldog with him wherever he went. I remember once he called to us and we all went outside the hotel and there he was, sitting up on the roof of a taxicab with the bulldog, waving at us."

That didn't bother Stallings as long as the zany Maranville produced on the field, as he usually did. Maranville didn't necessarily hit for high average, but he was dangerous with runners in scoring position.

"Do what you want but don't wind up in jail, and come to play every day," was Stallings's main message to his rowdy and raucous team.

Stallings, a pioneer in platooning, shuffled his players around like so many baseball cards. Nowhere was this truer than the outfield, where 11 players were used interchangeably in 1914 depending on the game situation. Getting the most work were left fielder Joe Connolly, center fielder Leslie Mann, and right fielder Larry Gilbert.

"I believe he was the first big-league manager to platoon outfielders," James remembered of Stallings. "He had a right-handed hitting outfield play the day a left-handed pitcher was going and a left-handed hitting outfield when a right-hander was opposing us."

As for the rest of the team, Stallings didn't have to worry too much. Powerful Butch Schmidt was the Braves' full-time first baseman and part-time bodyguard, and Hank Gowdy was their starting catcher.

"We had a real team, no cliques," Deal recalled. "We fought the other teams, not ourselves. I remember once in Chicago, Heinie Zimmerman tried to steal second. Rabbit Maranville liked to push his head in making the tag. Heinie took a swing at little Rabbit and big Butch Schmidt ran over to take a swing at Heinie. Ol' Heinie ran around screaming bloody murder, wanting to fight someone, but not Butch Schmidt."

Gowdy had come up to the big leagues in 1910 with the Giants as a first baseman and was traded to the Braves the next season. For a couple of years, he bounced between Boston and the minors. His career turned around when he turned to catching in 1913. And in 1914, he was a regular in the Boston lineup.

Stallings would pick up other players in trades during the season, some of them cast-offs from other teams. Few teams were as busy as the Braves trying to find pieces of the puzzle.

"The Braves were a misfit bunch, a lot of kids and old-timers mixed in, guys other clubs had given up on, in some cases," Deal said.

Stallings was ever optimistic.

"Give me a club of only mediocre ability," he said, "and if I can get the players in the right frame of mind, they'll beat the world champions."

Little did he know at that time in the spring, when all hope in baseball springs eternal, that the Braves would eventually get that opportunity in the fall.

For now, Stallings was just trying to get the Braves off to a good start in the National League race. It wasn't easy.

By the time the Braves played Brooklyn in their home opener on April 23, they had already lost four of their first five games.

Nevertheless, an excited, boisterous capacity crowd of 7,500 packed the South End Grounds, the Braves' shabby, outdated ballpark on the corner of Walpole and Tremont. The fans went home happy and optimistic after watching Boston beat Brooklyn 9-1 behind Lefty Tyler.

Their optimism soon dissipated. As the season wore on, losses mounted for the Braves. They dropped 16 of their first 19 games and were having trouble getting any kind of consistent performances from their big-three starters.

On July 4, the Braves were in last place in the National League with a 26-40 record, a whopping 15 games off the pace of the league-leading Giants. "I have 16 pitchers and they're all rotten," Stallings lamented.

As of July 5, James had the only winning record at 7-6. Rudolph was 6-8 and Tyler 5-8.

The Braves weren't just last in the league, they couldn't even beat their minor-league farm team in Buffalo in an exhibition game. Losing to a "soap company team," in Evers's words, might have been the low point of the season for Boston.

The Braves were standing on a train platform after the 10-2 loss.

"Big-league ballplayers you call yourselves. Ha . . . you're not even Grade-A sandlotters," Stallings said with venom in his voice. "I'm ashamed of you."

Whatever chord Stallings struck in his proud players must have been a deep one, for they started winning. The Braves won 9 of 12, and when they woke up on the morning of July 19, they were still in last place but only 11 games behind the first-place Giants. They had cut 4 games off the lead of the suddenly struggling Giants. Stallings was in a far better frame of mind.

"Now we'll catch New York," he told his team confidently. "We're playing 30 percent better ball than any team in the league."

The Giants were not concerned. They knew the Braves would need to climb over seven teams to make the top—virtually impossible with only half the season left.

When Boston beat Cincinnati 3-2 with a three-run rally in the ninth inning on July 19, the Braves started to make the "impossible" climb. The Giants happened to be in Cincinnati on a day off and took in the game. When Rudolph ran into some old Giants teammates at their hotel, he told them of the Braves' serious intentions to challenge for the pennant.

"You're just wasting your time, Dick," the Giants told Rudolph.

However, the Braves' victory over the Reds had moved them out of last place into seventh. The next day they were in sixth place after beating Pittsburgh 1-0 behind Tyler. The following afternoon, they moved into fourth as Rudolph shut out the Pirates again, 6-0.

On July 22, James held the Pirates scoreless for the third straight game with a 1-0, 11-inning decision in the opener of a doubleheader. Although the Braves lost the second game, Tyler came back with a 2-0 shutout the following day—the Braves' fourth in five games against the Pirates.

Maranville literally used his head to help the Braves post one of the shutouts. With the score tied 0-0 in the ninth, the Braves had the bases loaded when Maranville stepped up to the plate.

"Get on somehow, even if you have to get hit," Stallings instructed his peppery little shortstop.

Babe Adams, the Pirates' pitcher, fired two straight strikes. At this point, Maranville inched closer to the plate and leaned into the next pitch.

He didn't make much of an attempt to get out of the way, if he made any attempt at all. Adams's pitch hit Maranville squarely in the forehead, and umpire Charlie Moran wasn't sure whether he should call him out for interference or have him take his base.

Finally, a Solomon-like decision from the umpire.

"If you can walk to first base, I'll let you get away with it," Moran said.

The slightly dazed Maranville did, forcing in the lead run. The Braves held the Pirates scoreless in the bottom of the inning and walked off with a 1-0 win.

Taking one for the team was one of many contributions by Maranville in Boston's sudden second-half surge. On August 6, he slammed a home run in the 10th inning to give the Braves a

5-4 victory over Pittsburgh and extend their winning streak to nine games. Then Maranville singled home the winning run in a 4-3, 10-inning decision over Cincinnati. In another game against the Reds, he had a double and two singles to back James's six-hit pitching for a 3-1 Boston win.

When the Braves pulled into New York's Polo Grounds for a crucial three-game series in mid-August, they were in third place, only 6½ games behind the league leaders.

In the Boston press, the Braves were big news along with reports from Europe of World War I and from Mexico of bandit hero Pancho Villa.

To make any headway against the Giants, the Braves needed to win at least two of three from the league leaders. A sweep would be sweeter.

That's just what they got. The topper was a brilliant performance by Tyler, who outpitched the great Christy Mathewson 2-0 in 10 innings in the final game of the series.

The Braves continued their torrid play and by August 23 had tied the Giants for first with a 59-48 record. By now the Braves had captured the imagination of an entire country with their scrappy, hard-nosed play. With the war in Europe on everyone's mind, Americans had a chance to turn to the sports pages and read about the more positive news of Boston's thrilling charge.

"The spirit that caught on was grand and I think that was largely responsible for our success," James said. "We had been a last-place club for so many years that we became sentimental favorites. There wasn't one park in the league where the fans didn't treat us like a home team. We drew more cheers than the town's own clubs.

"As we kept our pennant drive going, the fans really started to pull for us everywhere."

The National League's top spot was now up for grabs between the Braves, Giants, and St. Louis Cardinals. The Braves slipped back to third after losing to the Cardinals in the opener of a four-game series in late August but then moved up by sweeping a doubleheader from the Redbirds and concluding the series with another win.

Now the nation's baseball fans focused on the sizzling battle between the Braves and Giants. The teams took turns taking over first place as the season headed into September.

By that time, the Braves were sharing Fenway Park with the Red Sox, thanks to Sox owner Joseph Lannin. The Red Sox boss offered the Braves the use of Fenway for their remaining games—including the World Series, if that became a reality.

When the Giants arrived in Boston for a big Labor Day doubleheader, Fenway Park was jam-packed—and noisy, as usual.

Reported the *Boston Post*: "It was a typical Boston crowd. They yelled, they brought various noisemaking implements along with them to show their allegiance to the Braves and they used them with unabated fury. Their applause of good plays was deafening and came during practice sessions as well as the game."

The last reference was to Maranville, who entertained the crowd by taking throws from catcher Hank Gowdy and outfielder Joe Connolly while sitting on second base.

You could always expect the unexpected from Maranville, and the Boston fans got something else unexpected that day: a near riot in the second game of the twin bill.

After the Braves won the opener 5-4 behind Rudolph, the Giants were on their way to a 10-1 victory in the nightcap when Tyler hit Fred Snodgrass with a pitch. The Giants outfielder immediately threatened the Braves pitcher. When the fans booed Snodgrass, he made an obscene gesture in their direction. The disorderly crowd was ready to jump onto the field and tear Snodgrass apart, but police soon restored order and the game continued.

The next day, James outdueled the Giants' Rube Marquard, with Evers lashing three hits. Scoring four times in the fourth inning, the Braves went on to an 8-3 victory and into first place one more time.

This time they didn't leave.

Pitchers continued to carry the Braves, even pitchers nobody ever heard of. Hoping to give his overworked staff a bit of a rest, Stallings brought in George "Iron" Davis, a Harvard law student with no professional baseball experience. All Davis did was pitch a no-hitter against the Philadelphia Phillies in the second game of a doubleheader.

It seemed the Braves could do no wrong at that point. And on September 29, they completed a 4-game sweep of Chicago and clinched their first National League pennant. That sweep gave the amazing Braves a 9-game lead over the Giants, which they expanded to 10½ by season's end.

Talk about torrid. From July 4 until the end of the season, the Braves had a 68-19 record.

Two of the "rotten" pitchers that Stallings complained about in the first half of the season—James and Rudolph—each won 26 games. From July 6 to October 6, James (19-1) and Rudolph (20-2) had a combined record of 39-3. Add Tyler's second-half performance of 11-5 and the big three had a combined mark of 50-8 in that time period. It would be hard to believe that any top three pitchers on one team in the history of baseball ever reached those dizzying heights following midseason.

However, the Braves were expected to come down to earth in the World Series against the powerhouse Athletics.

The A's boasted a strong pitching staff that spread the wealth. Led by Chief Bender's 17 victories, the well-balanced staff featured seven pitchers with double-digit wins. Along with Bender, the staff had Eddie Plank, Herb Pennock, Bob Shawkey, and Bullet Joe Bush.

The A's also had the $100,000 Infield, so named for the staggeringly high salaries that Mack paid these four starters. No infield unit in baseball came close.

Philadelphia's famed infield featured Stuffy McInnis at first base, Eddie Collins at second, John Barry at short, and Frank "Home Run" Baker at third. Baker led the American League with nine home runs in an era where homers were scarce. He was a future Hall of Famer, along with Collins, Plank, Bender, and Pennock.

The A's were generally regarded as 2-to-1 favorites to win the Series. Some gamblers were offering as much as 7-to-1.

Bender, the A's starter in Game 1, was supremely confident, so much so that instead of scouting the Braves, he had gone fishing the day before the opener at Shibe Park in Philadelphia.

"Who wants to scout a bush league team?" he said.

The "bush league team" gave Bender all he could handle—and more. The Braves knocked Bender out in the sixth inning and went on to a 7-1 win behind Rudolph's sharp five-hitter and a single, double, and triple by Gowdy. It was the first time the A's ace had been knocked out of a World Series game in 10 appearances.

As was his practice at the start of some big occasion, Stallings was wearing a newly purchased outfit for the game for good luck. When he returned to his hotel after the opening victory over the A's, he bundled up his underwear, shirt, socks, and suit and handed them all to his son.

"Here," he said, "take these down to the hotel laundry and have them washed and the suit pressed. Stay with them until they're finished, and then bring them back here and lock them in the closet."

George Stallings Jr. remembered in later years:

"I knew he had made up his mind that these clothes were lucky and that he would explode if anything happened to them. So from then on, I was special valet to the wardrobe."

With his nervous habit of sliding up and down on the bench, Stallings was already starting to wear the seat of his pants thin in Game 2 while watching James hook up in a pitching duel with Plank.

The Braves and A's were locked in a scoreless tie after eight innings. In the ninth, Deal opened with a double, stole third, and scored on Mann's single. Final: 1-0, behind James's two-hitter.

"By this time the betting had shifted," Gowdy once recalled. "Fans all over the country were pulling for the Braves."

To the shock of the entire baseball community, Stallings's upstarts were headed back to Boston with a 2-0 lead in the Series.

"We won't be coming back," a confident Stallings said before the game. "It'll be all over after two games in Boston."

But not so fast. . . .

In Game 3, the Braves appeared to hand the game to the A's when an error by Evers allowed two runs to score in the top of the 10th. That gave the A's a 4-2 lead and considerably quieted the sellout crowd at Fenway Park.

But in the bottom of the inning, Gowdy homered in the gathering darkness of a late October afternoon, and Connolly hit a sacrifice fly to tie the game at 4.

James, who had pitched a complete game just two days before, came on in the 11th to relieve Tyler. He gained his second victory within three days as Gowdy led off with a double in the 12th, and pinch runner Mann eventually scored on a bunt misplayed by A's pitcher Bush.

The 5-4 victory in the longest Series game played to that

Action during the 1914 World Series, in which the Boston Braves pulled off what was voted by sports writers in 1950 as "the greatest sports upset of the 20th century."

point lifted the hard-to-believe Braves within one game of the world championship.

It wasn't so hard to believe for Stallings, who said, "If we can win this game, we can't possibly lose tomorrow."

Stallings was so confident that his Braves would complete the four-game sweep that he canceled the team's train reservations back to Philadelphia.

With 34,365 roaring fans looking on at Fenway, that's just what the Braves did. Rudolph scattered seven hits, and Evers, the National League MVP, singled home two runs in the fifth to give the Braves a 3-1 victory.

Gowdy was the batting hero with a .545 average and five extra-base hits as the Boston Braves won their first and, as it turned out, only world title. Rudolph was the pitching hero, allowing only one run in 18 innings.

So the double-miracle season went into the books, never again matched in any shape or form in Boston Braves history. The Braves in Boston would make only one other World Series appearance, losing to Cleveland in 1948 before the franchise moved to Milwaukee.

After having one of the greatest second halves of any pitcher in baseball history, James pitched only two more years in a career interrupted by World War I, winning five of nine decisions. Rudolph pitched nine more seasons with the Braves but never approached his performance of 1914, finishing with a 122-108 career record. Tyler, the other member of the big three, pitched seven more seasons and finished with the Cubs. He posted a 127-119 mark in 12 years in the big leagues.

Stallings managed six more years in Boston, never again approaching the success of the 1914 team. He managed in the big leagues through 1920, when his Braves team finished in seventh place. His career record: 731 wins, 733 losses.

In 1950 a nationwide poll of sports writers picked the Braves' world championship season as the greatest sports upset of the 20th century.

"There never was another man like Stallings, and there never was another team like the 1914 Braves," Gowdy said.

# 4

## BUSTED IN TOKYO

As sacrificial lambs go, Buster Douglas was a meaty one. And, as the Japanese liked to claim, Mike Tyson was the second coming of Godzilla.

Douglas was such a rank outsider, with four losses on his unspectacular resume, that the smart guys in Las Vegas rated him anywhere from a 42-to-1 to 45-to-1 underdog for the February 11, 1990, bout in Tokyo. At a fleshy 231½ pounds, Douglas was an enticing main course for Iron Mike, who planned to then move on to more high-profile defenses of his heavyweight crown against Evander Holyfield and the resurrected George Foreman.

"Buster Douglas?" Tyson said, scorn dripping from every syllable. "Do you think Buster Douglas is going to beat me? Does Buster Douglas think he is going to beat me?"

Perhaps not. Tyson was 37-0 with 33 knockouts, and most of his opponents didn't make it out of the first round when the 23-year-old Tyson was at his most fearsome in the ring.

Douglas came in with a 29-4-1 mark, few of the wins particularly impressive. He'd been knocked out three times, and in his previous title attempt against the mediocre Tony Tucker in 1987, he put out such a poor showing that some expected him to disappear from boxing altogether.

Boxing writers took to calling him BUSTer DOGlas.

This was such a mismatch that promoter Don King couldn't sell it to a U.S. site, instead taking the Tyson Theater of the Absurd to the far east for the bout.

"This is just another small step for Mike Tyson on his way to the greatest career in heavyweight boxing," King blathered on . . . and on.

The next step would be something in the neighborhood of a $70 million meeting with Holyfield, so King considered Douglas nothing more than an annoying gnat Tyson would swat away with ease. And the promoter treated Douglas that way.

"It was obvious he wasn't neutral," Douglas said. "It was clear who he was rooting for."

It would become even clearer during the fight.

There was some evidence, however, that Douglas could at least present a minuscule challenge to Tyson, who came to Tokyo out of shape and with his mind cluttered by nonboxing matters, most of them dealing with the women in (and out of) his life and his penchant for spending far more cash than he had available.

Douglas was tall at 6-4, and his reach was 84 inches, almost unheard of in the heavyweight ranks. Indeed, only Jess Willard and Sonny Liston, two established champions of the past, had longer reaches.

So maybe Tyson, who stood about 5-10 and weighed 220, would have difficulty getting inside to land his bazooka-like shots.

Douglas also knew how to use his jab and how to slide away from danger. That could frustrate Tyson.

And there was something else: While Tyson's sense of purpose seemed dimmed, Douglas's was all too clear. His mother died three weeks before the fight, but instead of postponing his meeting with Tyson—and perhaps never getting his chance to be obliterated by Iron Mike—Douglas trained harder and showed more dedication to his sport than ever.

"Once I signed to fight him I knew that I could beat him," Douglas said.

At the time, Douglas actually felt more secure inside a boxing ring than he did outside of it.

"I was going through a lot in my life," he said. "My wife and I were separated, and it was just really bad outside of my boxing career.

"And then, of course, it intensified as my mom passed."

Before she did, she had visited Buster in Tokyo to check on him.

"From that point on she was confident I was prepared to fight. It was a trying time, but through the grace of God, I made it through all the things I was going through. There I was, preparing for one of the biggest nights of my life, and then all the things in my life were going bad.

"But I still stayed focused and was able to lean on boxing to bring me through that storm. It really was a difficult time in my life, but boxing helped me make it through because it took my mind off . . . my personal life. So he [Tyson] was the least of my worries."

The least of his worries? Tyson had disposed of better opponents in a matter of seconds.

But there were signs an upset could happen. During lackluster training sessions, Tyson had been floored by sparring partner Greg Page, a former heavyweight champion but nothing more than a pedestrian fighter at this juncture. Iron Mike even was cut once during sparring.

His longtime trainer, Kevin Rooney, had been fired by Tyson's growing entourage of hangers-on and glad-handers. In his place was a relative novice, Aaron Snowell, who was unable to get Tyson focused on his work. Managers such as Rory Holloway were too busy partying to pay attention to such woes.

"I'm not really concerned by the knockdown and the sluggish workouts; by all rights Mike should take Douglas out within two rounds," Rooney told *New York Times* sports columnist Dave Anderson. "But it shows Mike's got a bunch of amateurs around him."

And those amateurs were counting on Douglas being as unprepared for the fight as, well, their undedicated man.

"Douglas has a reputation for never having trained very hard," said Bill Cayton, Tyson's former manager. "But a well-trained Douglas could well be a different opponent."

Still, the journeyman Douglas beating the mighty Tyson? Come on.

"It was Tyson, Tyson, Tyson, everywhere you went," Douglas said. "And rightly so. You can't take away from the man what he had accomplished. He was the heavyweight champion of the world, and he had beaten everyone they put in front of him. Beat 'em bad. Real bad. I understood why they were doing what they were doing."

Douglas, 29, claimed he never watched Tyson live, even though he was on the undercard of three of Tyson's defenses. But he surely knew of Tyson's power, which had disposed of Michael Spinks, Frank Bruno, and Carl Williams in previous bouts.

The fight would take place midday to position it in the usual late evening time slot back in the United States for the HBO television audience. The cable network was preparing for a short program.

# CINDERELLA MAN

Generations of Americans post–World War II had little idea who James Braddock was. Indeed, until Russell Crowe portrayed him in the 2005 film *Cinderella Man*, Braddock's story was left to be told infrequently by boxing historians.

That's a shame because Braddock's upset of Max Baer was one of the biggest in sports history, and Braddock's journey to that title is among the most inspiring.

In the 1920s, Braddock was a formidable fighter who won several amateur titles before turning pro under manager Joe Gould. He went 36 fights without a defeat, and when Braddock first faced a real contender, light heavyweight Pete Latzo, he broke Latzo's jaw in a decisive victory.

Later in 1928, he knocked out undefeated Tuffy Griffith in two rounds. That led to a bout with champion Tommy Loughran in which Braddock was beaten badly, his hands damaged in the match.

Soon, Braddock was losing fight after fight. As the Great Depression hit America, Braddock's career already was on the skids. And much of his money was lost when the bank holding it failed.

Braddock couldn't find much work, taking jobs on the docks of New Jersey whenever they became available. He'd walk three or more miles daily to the shipyards, with no guarantee of work. He also applied for relief so he could feed his wife, Mae, and three children.

At 29, seemingly washed up, Braddock had only one boxing man still interested: Gould. Even though Gould also was struggling financially—who wasn't in those days?—he remained well connected in the sport.

Gould convinced Jimmy Johnston, the matchmaker at Madison Square Garden, the mecca of boxing, to place Braddock on the undercard of the Primo Carnera-Max Baer heavyweight title fight. The Garden sought an easy mark for rising heavyweight John "Corn" Griffin. A victory by Griffin would earn him a shot at the Carnera-Baer winner.

For $250, a pittance for most boxers but a godsend for Braddock, the desperate fighter was expected to get a severe whipping from Griffin. Braddock hadn't fought in nine months and hadn't won anything memorable in years.

But on June 14, 1934, a trim-looking Braddock entered the ring at Madison Square Garden Bowl in Queens, an outdoor facility frequently used for boxing.

"I was in great shape from the heavy work on the docks and from exercise and walking," Braddock said. "I was ready that night, even if no one except my family and Joe thought I was."

Ready for what? The beating of his life?

Well, no.

Griffin did hurt Braddock in the first round, and Braddock was knocked down in the second. Amazingly, he got up and immediately landed a sharp right hand, knocking down the young contender. Moments later, Griffin was barely hanging on, and the fight was stopped in the third round.

"I knew I had it in me," Braddock said.

In the main event, Baer sent Carnera to the canvas 11 times in a brutally one-sided bout for the belt. That overshadowed Braddock's victory somewhat, but Braddock was a name again in boxing circles.

After two more impressive wins, Braddock climbed to No. 2 in the rankings, but he was No. 1 among boxing fans. His story became so well known that famed sports writer Damon Runyon coined the nickname Cinderella Man for Braddock.

No longer on relief or working on the docks, and now able to feed, clothe, and house his family, Braddock set about going after the heavyweight crown. When a fight between Baer and top contender Max Schmeling could not be arranged, Baer signed to fight Braddock.

One day less than a year after his win against Griffin, Braddock was back in the MSG Bowl stadium, fighting for the most prestigious individual title in sports: HEAVYWEIGHT CHAMPION OF THE WORLD.

Most experts rated Braddock's chances as "infinitesimal." Baer, a noted playboy who abhorred training, took his opponent lightly, several times calling Braddock "a bum."

"I may not be a great fighter, but I ain't a bum," replied Braddock, who'd been through many more-challenging obstacles.

Baer was as much an entertainer as a fighter, and early on he clowned it up in the ring against Braddock, who was all business. When Baer was serious, he could hit and hurt Braddock. He simply wasn't serious very often, and Braddock's determination was obvious.

After Braddock won most of the early rounds, Baer became frustrated when he landed loaded punches, only to see Braddock come back for more. Baer stopped clowning once he realized he was being outpointed.

It was too late. Unless he could knock out Braddock, Baer would lose his belt.

But he couldn't knock out Braddock. Not even close. Indeed, in the 15th and final round, it was the challenger, the man of the people, the Cinderella Man, who was doling out the most punishment.

The judges' decision was unanimous. Runyon and other journalists of the day declared Braddock the most popular champion in the sport. Gould hugged Braddock harder than Baer had hit him.

Braddock understood that this would be the pinnacle of his career. Still, boxing had rescued him and his family. It was more than enough.

So was Tyson—he'd been doing so for weeks.

"No way I can lose," he said. "It will be quick and painful."

Painful, indeed. But not for Douglas.

And hardly quick.

Many of Tyson's knockout wins came because he so greatly intimidated an opponent before the fight. Douglas was unafraid. From the outset, he beat Tyson to the punch with sharp jabs that kept the hulking champion off balance, unable to load up his robust repertoire of bombing uppercuts and hooks.

When Tyson couldn't dispose of someone early, he tended to get sloppy. His technique never was particularly advanced—

not many sluggers can stick and dance, after all. His mind-set was simple: Move forward relentlessly, and bully your way to victory.

Douglas was not being bullied.

It was more of the same through the next few rounds. By the fifth, Tyson was so frustrated that he'd abandoned any game plan he might have developed for Douglas. In his corner, there was chaos; instead of offering encouragement or plotting strategy, Snowell and his seconds appeared dumbfounded. They didn't seem to know how to handle the swelling on Tyson's face let alone tell their fighter how to deal with the man who was on his way to taking the heavyweight championship.

Many fans in the Tokyo Dome sensed Tyson was in trouble. A buzz that began when Douglas not only escaped the first round but also won it became an uproar by the fifth round.

Even worse for the Tyson camp, Douglas knew he was in control.

"Probably about the fifth round or so, you could see he was having trouble," Douglas said. "Quite a few [opponents] got out of the first round with Mike. But after three rounds, four rounds, five rounds—he took a real good look at me, after about the fifth; you know, one of those kinds of expressions."

While Douglas understood that just one solid connection by Tyson could change the direction of the bout, he also believed Tyson would never make that connection. Douglas had cut the line.

"I was very sure of myself," Douglas said later. "I had been to the big show once before, when I fought Tucker, and I felt like I had seen it all. It was a sort of a 'been there, done that,' type of thing. People picked me to win that Tucker fight, and I wound up losing, but I learned from that. And even though basically nobody was picking me against Tyson, I knew what to expect, and I felt like I had what it took."

And he was using whatever it took.

Seated at ringside was Donald Trump, who expected to dig deep into his vaults for the front money to stage Tyson-Holyfield. With him was Dr. Elias Ghanem of the Nevada Athletic Commission, a supervisor for the World Boxing Council.

"I got there a few days before the fight, and the Tyson camp was so confident, it was like they couldn't believe Mike Tyson was capable of losing," Ghanem said. "They all kept saying, '45-second fight, 45-second fight.' I remember Rory [Holloway] kept yelling that over and over, and it was obvious they didn't put much into this fight.

"When I was talking with Donald, he was telling me about the $12 million site fee he was going to pay to have Tyson and Holyfield in Atlantic City. But as the fight was going on, he leaned over to me and said, 'Well, maybe I'll save that $12 million.'"

By the eighth round, Tyson's air of invincibility was shattered. His face was a mess, and his attacking style had slowly eroded to a plodding death march. In fact, Douglas, the supposed slacker, appeared to be gaining strength, and his marksmanship was withering the champ. Iron Mike was turning into tin.

Then it happened.

In the dying seconds of the eighth, Douglas got careless. Immediately, he found out that a weakened Tyson still is dangerous.

Tyson landed a right uppercut that floored Douglas with four seconds to go in the round. In a heavyweight title fight, the count keeps going when a fighter is on the canvas, even if the bell is supposed to sound.

More stunned than hurt, Douglas listened as veteran referee Octavio Meyran of Mexico began his count. Unaware that

Meyran began his count three seconds after the timekeeper, Douglas did exactly what any boxer is trained to do. He watched the ref, and when the count reached eight, he was on his feet, ready to resume.

The bell rang and Tyson's handlers, plus King, began a rant that would last a few weeks. They felt the fight was over and Douglas had been knocked out, even though Meyran never reached 10.

"I wasn't hurt and I heard him counting six, seven, eight," Douglas said.

"I just want fair play," Tyson later countered. "I thought legitimately he was out."

Meyran said otherwise, and the referee is the sole arbiter in such situations. The fight went on.

The crowd, now as frenzied as the well-behaved Japanese fans ever get, expected Tyson to finish the job in Round 9. So did Snowell, Holloway, and the rest of the Tyson brigade. So did Iron Mike.

"I went down because I was admiring what I was doing to him and he caught me a good shot," Douglas said. "If I just went back to what I'd been doing when he came charging out in the ninth, I figured he'd lose confidence he got from the knockdown and I'd have him."

As soon as the round began, it was as if Tyson's uppercut never landed. Douglas was fresh, sharp, and aggressive. Tyson was flabbergasted.

The 9th was among the best rounds of the night for Douglas. The 10th would be the best of his career.

After repeatedly landing hard blows to Tyson's head in the 9th, Douglas met little resistance from the champ in the 10th. Using his right hand with great effect, Douglas put together a five-punch combination that floored Tyson.

His left eye a bare slit from all the pounding, his face contorted as much in confusion as pain, Tyson searched for his mouthpiece, which Douglas had knocked out of Tyson's mouth and onto the canvas. Iron Mike found it, stuck it back in his mouth the wrong way, and was counted out for the first time.

The ring and its surroundings were sheer bedlam. Nobody had expected this.

King sought out the chiefs of the three boxing federations that sanctioned the fight—the World Boxing Council, World Boxing Association, and International Boxing Federation—asking that the verdict be overturned because Douglas received a long count from Meyran.

"The first knockdown obliterated the second," he claimed loudly.

King even got the WBC and WBA to temporarily withhold recognition of Douglas's victory. To its credit, the IBF wasn't swayed by King's twisted logic.

"He won the fight in the ring," IBF president Bob Lee said. "All he has to do is get up by the count of 10. If the clock doesn't work or the referee makes a mistake, it's not his fault."

The battered Tyson instructed the media: "Let me tell you something because you guys know I never bitch. I knocked him out before he knocked me out. Now you guys know I always walk it like I talk it."

On this night, though, it was Buster Douglas who did the walking, the talking, the hitting, and the winning.

"If Tyson was true to himself he would give me credit that I kicked his ass," Douglas said. "He's talking it, but no way he's walking it. This is cornball stuff, ludicrous. He's a baby. The whole world knows what happened to him in that 10th round. Suddenly he wasn't Superman anymore."

Tyson soon would back off such comments, crediting Douglas with a brilliant performance. But Douglas's reign would be short, while Tyson eventually would get back the title.

Eight months after his epic win, the magnitude of the upset would crystallize when a blimpy Douglas earned $20 million for a third-round loss to Holyfield. Douglas put up little resistance and barely was heard from afterward.

# 5

## AMBUSHING THE CADETS

On the night of December 2, 1950, a bell rang incessantly on the campus of the Naval Academy in Annapolis, Maryland.

A handful of midshipmen were banging away at the "Japanese Bell," signifying a win over Army in their annual football clash. The merry midshipmen said they would be "on duty" all night ringing that bell.

"It seems silly," one of them said, shivering in the cold, "but it hasn't been rung in so long."

Indeed. The victory over Army was the first time that Navy had won in the series since 1943.

More surprising: Navy was a 21-point underdog in this one.

A team sports rivalry like no other, the Cadets and Middies have taken turns knocking off each other at the most unpredictable times. But the topper of all the upsets might have been the 1950 game.

"Somebody must have mixed up the uniforms," wrote Bill Corum in the *New York Journal American*.

How shocking was it? Check this out:

◆ Army was 8-0, riding a 28-game unbeaten streak and ranked No. 2 in the country. With a 2-6 record in 1950, and 7-34-3 dating back to 1946, Navy was going through one of the leanest periods in its football history.

◆ The Cadets had won the previous year's game 38-0, at that time the biggest margin of victory in the rivalry.

◆ Earl Blaik was in the prime of his superb coaching career at Army, while Navy had a rookie head coach in Eddie Erdelatz, just getting his feet wet in Army-Navy action.

By now, Blaik was a bona fide coaching legend. He was a former Army assistant and the head coach at Dartmouth before taking over the Cadets' football program in 1941. The Cadets were down on their luck, and Blaik immediately turned them into winners, and ultimately, champions.

Going into the 1950 game with Navy, his teams in the previous six seasons had lost a total of two games, both in 1947 after the departure of the Doc Blanchard-Glenn Davis dynasty.

Mr. Inside (Blanchard) and Mr. Outside (Davis) made up one of the great running combinations in college football history, each winning the Heisman Trophy. They were largely responsible for national championships in 1944, 1945, and 1946, when the Cadets went a combined 27-0-1. The only imperfection on their record was a scoreless tie with a superb Notre Dame team in 1946, one of the greatest games in college football annals.

Following a 5-2-2 record in 1947, Blaik had the Army program back on top with undefeated seasons in 1948 and 1949. There were no Blanchards and Davises during this time, but Army featured solid, well-balanced teams that didn't give a yard. And as usual, the Cadets had some players on the All-American list.

In 1948, halfback Bobby Stuart and guard Joe Henry were selected to the All-American first team. In 1949, it was quarterback Arnold Galiffa. And in 1950, Army featured four first-team All-Americans in end Dan Foldberg, linebacker Elmer Stout, and defensive tackles Charles Shira and J. D. Kimmel.

Meanwhile, Erdelatz was brought in to turn things around at Navy, but his first season could hardly be called memorable. Before taking on Army, Erdelatz's Middies had already lost more games than they had under George Sauer in 1949.

"There is no hotter spot in sports than the coach's seat on either bench at an Army-Navy football game," wrote one newspaper, "and the record of recent years has made the job twice as tough at Navy as at Army."

If he felt the pressure, Erdelatz did not show it. A man with a good sense of humor, he could outquip Blaik, if nothing else.

Talking to reporters about his football days and college life at little St. Mary's (California), Erdelatz was asked: "What did you take at St. Mary's?"

"The morning paper," he responded.

Erdelatz had left an assistant coach's job with the San Francisco 49ers to come to Navy. With him he brought the 49ers' T-formation, a combination of 50 percent passing and 50 percent running.

"We may make Bob Zastrow run with the ball more to give our offense more variety," Erdelatz said of the Navy quarterback at a luncheon with reporters before the start of the season.

Despite mounting losses during the year, Erdelatz managed to keep his sense of humor.

Before the Army-Navy game, Blaik expressed indignation over Army's No. 2 ranking in the national polls. Blaik told reporters the Cadets deserved to be No. 1 instead of Oklahoma.

Upon hearing this, Erdelatz made this tongue-in-cheek observation:

"We're burned up, too," he said. "We're ranked number sixty-fifth and we should be sixty-fourth."

Seriously, Blaik had a point. The Cadets rolled into the Navy game after routing their eight opponents by an average score of 33-4. The Cadets not only were the top rushing team in the country but also boasted one of the best defenses. They had shut out five teams and allowed a combined total of only 26 points overall.

By contrast, the Middies had allowed their first eight opponents to score 174 points. And of the 101,000 spectators at Philadelphia's Municipal Stadium, including President Harry Truman, there couldn't have been any logical-thinking fans who believed Navy had even the slightest chance to beat Army.

Of course, logic never entered into the Army-Navy rivalry, which basically invented the familiar expression "You can throw out the records when these teams meet."

Before the game, an 813-foot "good luck" telegram arrived in the Navy locker room. It was signed by 824 midshipmen.

Then a smiling Truman posed with captains Foldberg of Army and Tom Bakke of Navy. A football game was a welcome relief for the president, who had been dealing with serious international problems: a war in Korea and a power struggle with General Douglas MacArthur over how that war should be handled.

That wasn't the only thing on Truman's mind. Just a month before, Puerto Rican nationalists tried to shoot their way into Blair House in an attempt to assassinate the president.

"The President and his party traveled from Washington under exceptional security precautions, with the Secret Service, local officials and the Pennsylvania railroad duplicating safeguards that were last used in the war," the *New York Times* reported.

Throughout the game, two Air Force F-51 fighters circled the stadium. They were guarding against intrusion by any aircraft that might threaten President Truman. Once, when a small plane flew across the field for what appeared to be a picture-taking junket, it was quickly chased away by one of the fighter planes.

Probably because of security concerns, Truman didn't attempt to change sides at halftime as presidents usually do. He sat throughout on the Navy side—the Middies were the designated "home team" for the game.

If either the oversized telegram or Truman's position in the stands proved to be good luck charms for Navy, it was hard to tell. It seemed that the Middies were making their own luck with their most ferocious defense of the season.

They set the tone right away on this bitterly cold December day. When the Middies fumbled the ball early, setting up great field position for the Cadets on the Navy 22, they merely stopped Army cold on four downs. Remember, this was the same Navy team that lost to Maryland 35-21, to Pennsylvania 30-7, and to Tulane 27-0.

The Middies were huge underdogs, but they weren't playing as though they knew it. And when given a similar turnover opportunity by the Cadets in the second period, Navy cashed in.

The Middies had the ball on the Army 27 after falling on a Cadets fumble. Quarterback Zastrow finished a short drive by weaving 7 yards through the middle of the Army defense for a 7-0 Navy lead.

When the Middies next got the ball in the period, they drove 63 yards in just five plays. Zastrow completed the drive with a 30-yard pass to Jim Baldinger, who made a leaping catch in the end zone. For the second time in the game, Zastrow held on the point after, literally giving him a hand in every Navy point.

The stunning halftime score: Navy 14, Army 0.

Even more stunning, Army managed only one first down in the entire half and only 3 yards of offense. Army's running attack had been averaging 312 yards a game.

Army's offense did a little better in the second half but still couldn't get the ball in the end zone. The Cadets advanced the ball seven times inside Navy's 20-yard line in the third and fourth quarters but came away empty-handed each time. The Cadets' only score came when the defense trapped Zastrow in the end zone, giving them two points.

Final: Navy 14, Army 2.

It wasn't just the score but the way the Middies dominated that was so stunning. Navy led in first downs (13-5) and in total yardage (268-139).

Navy defenders forced Army to fumble five times—more than the Cadets had given away in the previous eight games combined!

The Middies intercepted five passes by quarterback Bob Blaik, the coach's son. That, too, surpassed the total interceptions against Blaik for the entire season. When the Middies weren't picking off Blaik's passes, they were usually forcing him into bad throws or tackling him for losses behind the line.

The end of the game signaled a mad rush from the stands onto the field by the deliriously happy 3,700 midshipmen in Municipal Stadium that day.

The midshipmen stormed "down from the stands to raise Coach Erdelatz, Captain Bakke and their other heroes to their shoulders," wrote Allison Danzig in the *New York Times*.

Blaik gave the Navy coaching staff a lot of credit for the upset.

"We were well-scouted offensively," he told reporters.

Otherwise, he chalked it up to Navy spirit.

"They outcharged us . . . they overwhelmed us," he said.

Erdelatz, meanwhile, called it "the greatest team effort I've ever seen."

Erdelatz remained at Navy for seven more seasons, compiling a 39-11-1 record before becoming the first coach of the Oakland Raiders in the old American Football League.

In his time at Navy, he not only fulfilled his assignment of turning around the program but also had a good deal of success against Blaik. In nine meetings with the Old Master, Erdelatz came out on top 5-3-1.

It's obvious that neither would ever forget a certain meeting on December 2, 1950.

# 6

## THE AMAZIN' METS

For the first seven years of their existence, the New York Mets were the joke of baseball. In 1969, they finally delivered their own punch line.

The Baltimore Orioles didn't see it coming, nor did the rest of the baseball world.

Who would have thought it? The Miserable Mets suddenly became the Amazin' Mets, with a storybook season that finished with a World Series victory over the haughty Orioles.

Talk about coming out of left field—this was a real shock to the heavily favored Orioles.

Were the Mets "darlings of destiny," as one writer suggested? After all, they overcame 100-to-1 odds to win the National League pennant. And in the 1969 World Series, things just kept falling into place for the Mets—as if dictated by some higher power.

The Orioles were considered the best defensive team in

baseball. But it was the Mets who made the spectacular plays and the Orioles the misplays.

The Orioles had one of the best hitting teams around, packed with home run power. But it was the unheralded Mets hitting the long ball and producing in the clutch, as well.

Even umpires' decisions seemed to favor the New York team.

When the Series started in Baltimore, the Orioles didn't think they would get much trouble from the National League champions. Asked to predict the outcome of the Series, Orioles catcher Andy Etchebarren replied, "Four straight."

Third baseman Brooks Robinson admittedly was "not so charged up" as he was in his first World Series—a sweep of the Los Angeles Dodgers in 1966.

No wonder the Orioles felt that way.

In winning the American League's East Division title under manager Earl Weaver, the Orioles finished a whopping 19 games ahead of their closest competitors, the Detroit Tigers. The Orioles had won 109 games during the regular season before adding three more victories over West-champion Minnesota for the AL championship.

The Orioles looked just like what they were supposed to be: the best team in baseball.

"We dazzled 'em with our footwork in the first two games, then we knocked them out," Orioles outfielder Frank Robinson wisecracked, referring to two tense extra-inning victories over the Twins and then an 11-2 rout in the clinching third game.

Robinson, one of baseball's top sluggers with Cincinnati and now Baltimore, was a big cog in the Orioles' sweep of the Dodgers in the 1966 Series. And many of the players still remained from that championship team. This was a dynasty in the making.

The Orioles featured two 20-game winners in Mike Cuellar

and Dave McNally and no doubt would have had a third if Jim Palmer hadn't lost 41 days with a torn muscle in his back. As it was, Palmer won 16 games and lost only 4. The fourth starter, Tom Phoebus, posted 14 victories.

The Orioles also had depth in their bullpen with Eddie Watt and Pete Richert, among others. In an era when pitchers usually completed many of their games—Cuellar had 18 CGs, and McNally and Palmer 11 each—there weren't as many save opportunities for most relievers. Watt led the Orioles with 16 saves, while Richert had 12.

Not that the Mets didn't have a standout pitching staff led by Tom Seaver and Jerry Koosman among the starters and Tug McGraw in the bullpen. Seaver, a Cy Young candidate, had won 25 games and Koosman 17. If there was one area where the Mets could match up with the Orioles, it was their pitching. However, even there Baltimore had the edge in playoff experience and in ERA (2.83 to 2.99).

About the hitting, no contest—at least on paper.

With Donn Clendenon and Ed Kranepool sharing first base, the Mets certainly didn't have anyone at that position equal to Baltimore's Boog Powell. With 37 home runs, Powell had 10 more than Clendenon and Kranepool combined. With 121 RBIs, he exceeded the combined total of the Mets' two first basemen by 21. And with his .304 batting average, Powell couldn't even see Clendenon (.248) or Kranepool (.238) in the rear-view mirror.

The Orioles' other big RBI man, Frank Robinson, had knocked in 100 runs, 24 more than the leading Mets run-producer (center fielder Tommie Agee). Robinson's 32 homers had contributed to Baltimore's huge edge in team home runs (175 to 109) and batting average (.265 to .242).

Another element where the Orioles had the edge over the Mets was defense. The Orioles' infield was anchored by Brooks

Robinson, the best third baseman in baseball, and Mark Belanger, arguably the best defensive shortstop. Paul Blair was one of the smoothest center fielders in the game.

"Defensively, there isn't a weakness to be found," reported the *New York Times*. "Robinson . . . makes difficult plays look routine. . . . Blair catches everything from left-center to right-center."

Everyone knew about these Orioles and their big-name, big-time players. But who were these Mets, anyway, and what were they doing on top of the National League? They had come from as far down as possible, starting in 1962. In their first year as an expansion team, the Mets played 160 games. They lost 120 of them.

The 40-120 record may stand forever.

"Come and see my Amazin' Mets," manager Casey Stengel proclaimed, "which in some cases has played only semi-pro ball."

Those Amazin' Mets of 1962 finished last among the 10 National League teams, an unbelievable 60½ games behind the San Francisco Giants.

In the next six seasons, the Mets developed a reputation as "lovable losers" while playing for Stengel and, later, Wes Westrum. In succession, they lost 111, 109, 112, 95, 101 and 89 games. From 1962–1968, the Mets established a string of futility rare in major league baseball, finishing last five times and in ninth place on two other occasions.

"The Mets had spent so much time at the bottom," cracked one writer, "they were thinking of making the team emblem an anchor."

The Mets' hapless image was personified in "Marvelous" Marv Throneberry, a colorful first baseman prone to mishaps—both mental and physical.

In one game, Throneberry hit what appeared to be a triple. But he was called out for failing to touch first base.

An enraged Stengel flew out of the dugout to protest.

"Quiet down, Case," coach Cookie Lavagetto said as he intercepted the New York manager, "he didn't touch second base, either."

If there was a turning point in the Mets' fortunes, it was the hiring of Gil Hodges as manager in 1967. Hodges had been a star first baseman for the old Brooklyn Dodgers and later manager of the Washington Senators.

Hodges brought a firm hand to the Mets. Within two years he had survived a heart attack and led the team to first place. It was hard to believe, but the Mets actually won 100 games in 1969 to finish first in the National League East after finishing ninth the season before. And then they added three more victories in sweeping a series from the West-winning Atlanta Braves to win their first National League pennant.

"Lovable losers," no more. But could the Mets actually win the World Series, especially after losing the opening game to the Orioles, 4-1? And particularly after having Seaver, their ace pitcher, roughed up by Orioles batters?

On his second pitch of the game, Seaver gave up a home run to 5-foot-7 Don Buford, who had hit but 11 in 554 at-bats during the season. Then Seaver gave up three more runs in the fourth and left after five innings.

Cuellar, meanwhile, pitched a six-hitter as the Orioles cruised. Frank Robinson said the Mets looked "lifeless."

"I think we just took it out of them," he said. "They had their best pitcher going for them and a little guy, Don Buford, pops it out on him."

Heavy underdogs when the Series started, the Mets were even more so now.

"The most anonymous team ever to get in a World Series, they were like the understudy who finally gets her big chance and then forgets the lines," wrote Jim Murray in the *Los Angeles Times*.

The "understudy" turned into a star performer in Game 2, however. Koosman pitched the Mets to victory with last-out relief help from Ron Taylor, the only Met with World Series experience (1964 St. Louis Cardinals).

Talk about good theater. Koosman, backed by a home run by Clendenon and an RBI single by Al Weis, held a 2-1 lead in the ninth when he walked two hitters on 3-2 counts with two out.

In came Taylor to face Brooks Robinson, who had hit 23 home runs and knocked in 84 runs during the season.

"I knew I had to get Brooks out," Taylor said. "If not, we might go back to New York two games down."

Taylor had pitched four scoreless innings for the Cardinals against the New York Yankees in the 1964 Series. But he said, "This was the toughest one-on-one test for me."

With a 3-2 count, Robinson smashed Taylor's next pitch to third, where Ed Charles was playing deep. But after fielding the ball, Charles hesitated. He knew he couldn't outrace pinch runner Merv Rettenmund to the third base bag for the forceout. He recovered quickly and fired to first base, but his throw was in the dirt.

No problem. Clendenon made a nice pickup of the short-hop throw as the Mets tied the Series at a game apiece.

"Brooks is not the fastest thing on foot," Clendenon said. "So we had time to get him, even though the throw was a little low."

Next stop: Shea Stadium for Games 3, 4, and 5. And everyone get ready for "Metsomania." The Orioles, who had a less passionate fan base in Baltimore, prepared to meet a noisy madhouse in New York. The championship-starved Mets fans were among the most vocal in baseball. What the Orioles didn't expect was the silence of their own bats.

Game 3 went to the Mets, 5-0, as Agee made two remarkable game-saving catches in center field.

"He shut off five runs with a pair of catches that had to be seen to be believed," wrote Arthur Daley in the *New York Times*, "and even on instant replay it was exceedingly difficult to believe them."

Catch number one:

In the fourth inning, the Orioles trailed 3-0 but had two men on with two outs. Elrod Hendricks, a left-handed batter, smashed a drive off Gary Gentry toward the fence in left-center that looked like at least a double. Agee caught up with the opposite-field drive after a long run, stretched his glove as far as he could reach across his body, and made a sensational one-hand catch.

Catch number two:

In the seventh inning, the Orioles had the bases loaded with two outs when Blair poked a drive off Nolan Ryan to right-center, another "wrong-field" shot. Agee raced to his left, stretched out his glove in front of him, and made a miraculous diving catch as he skidded chest-first across the outfield grass.

"These were the plays of the day—the plays of the Series so far," reported the *New York Times*. "If any other catches in the history of baseball's Fall Classic were as good, or better, certainly no one ever followed one such act with another in the same game."

All but forgotten was the work Agee had also done with his bat. He led off the game with a 400-foot home run off Palmer, considered by the Orioles themselves to be their best pitcher.

Gentry, meanwhile, the Mets' third-best pitcher, not only outdueled Palmer, the Orioles' onetime "boy wonder," but also slugged a two-run double off him.

The Mets were feeling pretty good about their chances. They had their two best pitchers—Seaver and Koosman—lined up for the next games in New York.

In Game 4, Clendenon was starting to look like Frank Robinson with his second homer of the Series. And Seaver was looking more like himself after his poor performance in the opener.

The right-hander led 1-0 after eight innings, allowing only three hits to the powerful Orioles, who had been held scoreless only eight times in 162 games during the regular season.

But then in the ninth, Baltimore scratched out a run on singles by Frank Robinson and Powell and on Brooks Robinson's sacrifice fly. Ron Swoboda made a diving backhand catch in right field on Robinson's fly ball that was reminiscent of Agee's spectacular catches in Game 3.

"It's not a gamble," Swoboda said. "You either try to catch it or watch it roll to the fence. You say, let's go and get it."

In the 10th, the Mets caught a break. Buford momentarily lost Jerry Grote's leadoff fly ball to left in the bright sky, and it dropped for a double. Weis was walked intentionally, setting up a forceout at any base.

The managerial wheels started turning. Hodges sent up left-handed hitter J. C. Martin to bat for Seaver against the right-handed Dick Hall. Weaver countered with the left-handed Richert.

It was no secret what Martin was sent up to do: bunt the runners into scoring position for Agee, who had hit 26 home runs during the season.

Martin laid down a perfect bunt toward first base. Richert picked up the ball and fired to Davey Johnson, the second baseman covering the bag. However, the ball never reached Johnson. It glanced off Martin's left wrist and bounced into right field. Rod Gasper, pinch running for Grote, came roaring around third with the winning run in New York's 2-1 decision.

Nobody seemed to notice that the Mets had scored on an illegal play. Martin was running on the inside of the foul line, to the left of the base, which was prohibited according to Rule 6.05 (k): "A batter is out when . . . in running the last half of the distance from home base to first base while the ball is being fielded to first base, he runs outside (to the right of) the three-foot lane, or inside (to the left of) the foul line and in the umpire's judgment in so doing interferes with the fielder making his throw to first base."

It was later brought to light by an Associated Press photo showing Martin running on the inside to the left of the base.

However, providence once more seemed to be smiling down on the Mets as they took a 3-1 lead in the Series.

And the Mets caught some more breaks in Game 5.

The Orioles led 3-0 in the top of the sixth inning when Frank Robinson was hit by a pitch from Koosman. But umpire Lou Dimuro refused to award Robinson the base because he said the ball hit his bat first.

Robinson hotly disputed the umpire's call.

"I have never tried to decoy an ump when a ball hit my bat," the veteran outfielder would say later. "And I know it didn't hit the bat because I didn't feel it. I can tell when a ball hits my bat, even when it just nicks it."

Robinson struck out, and Powell followed with a single. Although Brooks Robinson lined to left for the third out, the umpire's decision did have a detrimental effect on the Orioles' inning.

"If Frank had been given the base," Weaver would later explain, "we'd have men on first and second with one out and

*Pandemonium breaks out as the improbable Mets take the Orioles in five games in the 1969 World Series.*

Brooksie at the plate. Brooksie didn't get a hit, but we still would have had one more chance."

It was a different story for the Mets in a similar situation in the bottom of the sixth.

A pitch got away from McNally and hit Cleon Jones's right shoe. Dimuro first ruled that the New York outfielder hadn't been touched by the pitch.

The Mets thought otherwise.

"The ball ricocheted off into our dugout and Jerry Grote caught it," Hodges said. "He looked at it and saw there was a mark on it. It was a distinctive mark, a shoe-polish mark."

Hodges walked out to home plate with the ball to show Dimuro evidence that his player had been hit by the pitch. Dimuro agreed, awarding Jones first base.

Clendenon followed with a home run to cut Baltimore's lead to 3-2.

Then in the seventh, the Mets tied the game on a home run from one of their most unlikely sources: Weis. Who would have figured that? Weis had never hit a home run before in Shea Stadium and had hit only two in 247 at-bats all season.

Darlings of destiny, indeed.

In the eighth, the Mets broke the 3-3 tie on doubles by Jones and Swoboda. Another run scored when the Orioles made two errors on one play.

Koosman made the lead stand, completing a five-hitter as the Mets beat the Orioles 5-3 to win the world championship.

"The Impossible Occurs" blared one headline over a photograph showing Hodges celebrating with Stengel.

The former manager had coined the expression "the Amazin' Mets" back when they were truly awful. It was meant as a denigrating remark then. But now Stengel could say it and actually mean it in a positive sense.

Amazin' indeed.

# 7

## RULON RULES

Rulon Gardner stood on the mat, so deep in concentration he didn't notice the frenzy around him.

The crowd at Exhibition Hall in Sydney, Australia, had come to see the coronation of Alexander Karelin, or more accurately, the recoronation. The Russian Greco-Roman wrestler hadn't lost a match in 13 years. The Siberian Bear had surrendered all of one point—one point—in the last decade!

Yet here stood Gardner, the farm boy from nowhere (actually, from Afton, Wyoming), on the verge of beating the unbeatable, of bringing down the one athlete considered invincible at the 2000 Olympics. Indeed, nearly everyone at the Sydney Games, from media to coaches to officials to, yes, even the athletes, expected Karelin's gold medal run to reach four.

But Gardner already had done the unthinkable—he scored against Karelin in the second period and led their championship match 1-0.

"I couldn't stop to think about scoring or being ahead,"

Gardner said. "I had an opportunity to win the match and that was all it meant. I couldn't abandon any of the things I was doing, because I knew how quickly he could turn it around. In seconds, you could be flat and out."

Karelin had been so dominant that former U.S. champion Matt Ghaffari likened facing him to "wrestling King Kong." Even though Ghaffari had once broken Karelin's rib in a match, he still was beaten by King Karelin.

"I didn't want to appear weak and skip a fight because of such a trifle as broken ribs," Karelin said of that match. "They would have to carry me out on a stretcher to quit."

Instead, it had been opponent after opponent who left the mat bruised, bloodied, and beaten. Karelin was as close to a foolproof victory-producing machine as anything the Russians had developed in their prolific Olympic history.

His training regimen was so structured that Karelin almost never took a day off. He would carry logs under his arms through the snow in Siberia to test his strength and his mettle. One story (myth?) had Karelin carrying a refrigerator on his back up seven flights of stairs to avoid having to ask for help.

When he looked directly at an opponent, he really was looking inside to measure what the enemy was made of. None of them had measured up.

At 6-3, 286 pounds, Karelin was so relentless that even in close matches the outcome rarely appeared in doubt. He might not have broken opponents' limbs, but he certainly broke their wills.

His trademark move was a reverse body lift that no other super heavyweights contemplated attempting. Several of Karelin's opponents, including two in the 1992 Barcelona Games, basically quit rather than take the chance they would be skylifted, then dumped and pinned by the Russian.

Once, very early in his career, Karelin used that move to win a match in which he trailed 3-0 with 30 seconds remaining. He scored 5 points for the reverse body lift to beat his Bulgarian opponent.

Ghaffari had come as close as anyone to succeeding against Karelin, losing in overtime at the 1996 Atlanta Olympics. It was one of 22 losses he sustained against the Russian champion.

"That guy ripped my guts out," Ghaffari said.

It had reached the point where a 1-0 or 2-0 Karelin victory almost was a disappointment.

"I know the weight of the world is on my shoulders now," he said in Sydney just before the wrestling event began. "But I should be used to it by now."

Gardner, on the other hand, didn't need to worry about pressure. While considered a medal contender after beating Ghaffari at the Olympic trials, the idea of this 29-year-old former Nebraska Cornhusker taking down the great Russian seemed absurd. Gardner talked a good fight, though.

"I'm here to take the torch," he said. "I want to step out and say, 'Hey, put Matt in the background. I want to be the man now.'"

While impressed by Karelin's record, the American wasn't overwhelmed by his background or his training regimen.

"I know it's cold in Siberia, but it can get to 40 below where I grew up, too," Gardner said of his Wyoming roots. "I don't know if it can get that much colder, even in Siberia."

Despite that kind of cold, Gardner, the youngest of nine children, worked his parents' farm each day, milking cows, then lifting frozen bales of hay to feed them.

"I would go out as a kid and I could barely pick up a bale of hay," Gardner recalled. "By the time my senior year came around, I was grabbing four bales of hay at a time, each 100 pounds, . . . and walking with them and seeing how physically strong I could be."

"It's twice a day, 365 days a year, 730 times a year, milking the cows and taking care of them," Reed Gardner, Rulon's father, told the Associated Press. "There are no days off in the dairy business. He had his jobs to do and he did them, every day. He would go to football practice or wrestling practice [at the high school], then come home and do his work."

So he went from an overweight kid called Fatso by some schoolmates to an all-state athlete who could have played football at Nebraska but chose wrestling.

Gardner's resume hardly compared with Karelin's, but he was no slouch heading to Sydney. He'd won two national championships and a Pan American Games gold medal.

He'd also been beaten by Karelin in 1997. He wasn't befuddled or intimidated by him, but it was understandable if Gardner wasn't overly optimistic, either.

"Realistically, I didn't think I actually could beat him," Gardner admitted. "The gold [medal] was so far away from what I thought I could do in my life. You say you can beat him, but so have so many people through the years in so many matches against this guy, then they go out and he crushes them.

"Even though I didn't think I was going to win, I was going to work as hard as I could," Gardner added. "If I didn't win, fine. But if I did, well, it's just incredible."

For the incredible to happen, Gardner needed a plan. As he marched toward the medal round, he couldn't think about Karelin too much. So before the Olympics began, he had formulated a scheme that, he claimed, could even things against the Siberian superstar.

Because Karelin, at 33, had slowed a bit, Gardner and the

U.S. coaches believed the best strategy was to force him into uncomfortable positions early in the match. Gardner might be able to sneak an early point and . . .

Wait a minute! Nobody had scored off Karelin in 10 years. He went through his earlier matches in Sydney without yielding a point, and now he was in the finals, facing the unheralded farm boy from Wyoming. This kid was going to dethrone King Kong?

"Ultimately I hoped to beat Karelin, but my chances in that match were really nothing to brag about," Gardner admitted. "I was just hoping and people were hoping I would get that chance to beat him."

In his semifinal match at the Olympics, Gardner was down 2-0 to Juri Yevseychyc of Israel but won 3-2 in overtime.

"Each match became closer and tougher, so it becomes a matter of mastering your ability as you win matches," Gardner said. "I felt I'd done that."

The match with Karelin was the second of the day for Gardner. It was the third for Karelin, which encouraged the American coaches.

"Karelin would never show it, but there could be some fatigue," coach Steve Fraser said of the man he once called the best wrestler in history. "Just enough to make a difference."

Before a crowd that included Henry Kissinger and IOC president Juan Antonio Samaranch—on hand, no doubt, to present Karelin with a fourth gold medal—the match was scoreless through one period. That meant the wrestlers would begin the second session in a clinch that would remain until one of them scored a point with a maneuver or one of them released his locked hands.

Gardner wanted this situation. He believed he could outlast Karelin in a clinch.

"He had a great lock on me, and another three or four

inches I would have let it slip," Gardner said. "But I always wrestle kind of unorthodox, and our feet got tangled and I got under him. Maybe it confused him. But I said to myself 'He broke,' and I got the point."

Indeed, Gardner took the lead when Karelin's hands separated.

From that juncture, everyone assumed Karelin would rally with a vengeance. Even Gardner believed it.

"A point is only one point," he said. "Hey, you scored a point against the best ever, but there were 5½ minutes left. The last thing I ever thought about accomplishing at that point was winning it. I was in against an athlete who had done the best for every day of his life."

Instead, Karelin faded. He rarely got Gardner into a position of danger, and although Gardner was not wrestling conservatively, the American wasn't coming close to scoring, either.

In the final minute, Karelin's visage changed, perhaps for the first time in his illustrious career. He seemed to realize he couldn't score, couldn't tie the match or surge ahead, couldn't capture yet another gold medal.

And in the dying seconds, the Russian dropped his hands in defeat.

"I wasn't coming out of my [wrestling] stance," Gardner noted. "Who knows what he's doing. Maybe as soon as I relax, he comes at me and throws me, or finds a way to score a point.

"But if he did that out of respect, then I really appreciate it. And to win that match the way I did was a shock. As an athlete you don't work your whole life to fail. There's no guarantee you'll be successful, but you never turn away from your goal."

Karelin only mumbled something in Russian as the referee lifted Gardner's hand, symbolizing what many would call "the miracle on the mat."

"I looked over and saw the Russians and saw the sadness

AFP/Getty Images

*Rulon Gardner celebrates following his shocking defeat of Russia's*
*Alexander Karelin at the 2000 Sydney Olympics.*

they had and that Karelin had in his face," Gardner said. "Each athlete has expectations upon their ability, and if you don't achieve your true potential, the frustration kicks in, and I think it turns to a level of just complete failure. An athlete works their whole life—and Karelin was the best ever—and to lose that match the way he did, there is nothing in your heart to help you understand it."

In these days of instant media, word of Gardner's shocker spread throughout Sydney and, quickly after, throughout the world. Yes, even back to Wyoming's Star Valley.

"We're on fire over here," said Richard Hoopes, Star Valley High School's athletic director. "We've already got a banner over Main Street under the Elkhorn Arch that says 'Home of Rulon Gardner, Olympic Gold Medalist.'"

Rulon Gardner, Olympic gold medalist. Imagine that.

"I kept saying that I think I can do it, but it wasn't until it was over that I knew I could," Gardner admitted. "The reason I think I won is because I work harder than anyone else, train harder. And every day I live my life, I do everything I need to do to put my life in order."

But his life would encounter much disorder after his monumental upset. While Karelin pretty much would fade from the scene, Gardner would face more daunting challenges over the next four years. So daunting that they would nearly cost him his life, would cost him a toe, and would make his journey back to the Olympics just as impressive as his gold medal stunner in Sydney.

Gardner carried the U.S. flag in the closing ceremony in Australia, then returned home to appear on all the major TV talk shows. He was eager to get back to Afton, where youngsters wore T-shirts with his picture on the front, "Miracle on the Mat" on the back. And when he returned, thousands showed up to welcome their conquering hero.

After riding into town on a fire truck, Gardner held up his gold medal and told the crowd, "This medal is not mine, this is all of ours.

"When I want to find happiness and find a place where I know everybody loves me," he added, "I come back home."

But he now was a man of the sporting world, and he would collect dozens of honors over the next few months, including U.S. Olympic Committee Sportsman of the Year and the Sullivan Award as the nation's top nonprofessional athlete. He would give motivational speeches at schools and churches, in

Fortune 500 and FFA meetings, at ballgames and wrestling competitions. The big boy from the little farming community was now a celebrity.

He also still was plain old Rulon, and he enjoyed being away from the spotlight. What better way to avoid the relentless attention than going off into the wilderness.

Gardner and several friends went snowmobiling one February afternoon when temperatures sneaked up toward the freezing mark, somewhat balmy in Wyoming for that time of year.

"Just a few hours of fun, because the weather was pretty good," he said.

But Gardner became separated from his companions when his snowmobile could not negotiate a ridge. Gardner began driving back to civilization—and got lost. Very lost. He crossed over the Salt River once, twice, three times. Each crossing soaked him to the bone. As the darkness enveloped Gardner, he quickly realized he could freeze to death if he didn't get drier and warmer.

"I tried to walk out, but the snow was four feet deep," Gardner said. "It was so cold I laid down on the ice in the river for 10 or 15 minutes. But I knew I had to get out of there or I was going to die."

But which way? Gardner had no clue.

The best he could do was trek toward a group of trees that might provide shelter from the icy wind and elements of what promised to be a bitterly cold—and long—night.

Already exhausted, he dug as deeply into the snow as he could to protect himself. He knew that a storm or a wandering animal looking for food would mean almost certain death. So would a lengthy sleep.

At one point, he thought he heard snowmobiles nearby. Or was it his imagination? He was too cold, too tired, and too weak to respond—if they were there at all.

Through the hours, as the temperatures plunged to 20 below zero, Gardner shivered, trying to alternate the position of his body to keep the circulation going. To stay alive.

"I'd put myself in a real awkward position so it would hurt and I'd wake up in five or 10 minutes," he told the Associated Press. "I would dream of starting a nice warm bath or shower. The worst part was I would wake up and find out I wasn't in that nice warm shower."

No, he was still out there, somewhere, in the deep, lonely darkness. And he knew if he made it until sunlight, rescuers would resume their searches.

An Olympic champion who stared down the great Karelin wasn't about to expire like this. Gardner's father would say that Rulon's fortitude, developed over the years on the wrestling mat and refined so magnificently in Sydney, was what saved him that night.

At daybreak, Gardner summoned enough energy to move into the sunlight. By then, he was too disoriented to hear or locate any rescue parties.

But they were out there. A pilot spotted Gardner and dropped him a coat, but the wrestler didn't respond.

A helicopter came to the spot where Gardner lay, its occupants uncertain if they'd found a breathing survivor or a corpse.

Barely alive, with a body temperature of 88 and frostbite on his limbs, Gardner was airlifted to a hospital in Idaho Falls, Idaho. He'd spent 17 hours battling the elements.

"Rulon is a fighter," Reed Gardner said. "He wasn't going to lose that fight, either."

Gardner spent nearly two weeks hospitalized and was in and out of hospitals for months. He lost the middle toe of his right foot, but, almost miraculously, nothing else.

Except, it seemed, his wrestling career. At 30, with another

Olympics just more than two years away, Gardner appeared finished on the mat.

"I wasn't willing to give up on my dreams," he protested. "The dream to wrestle for me is part of why I live and what I live for."

So, ever the optimist, Gardner's view of his lost night was not of a loss at all.

"I don't think of that as a horrific night," he said. "I think of that as an opportunity. What an opportunity, what an experience in my life. Say you put yourself through something so horrific and make it through that experience. What can't you face and come out of if you do that? How many of us come out of a life and death situation like that? If you think about it, I should have been dead."

So returning to topflight wrestling would be, well, like a walk in the park.

Even if the doctors were saying otherwise. They warned that his balance never would be the same, and in wrestling, balance is as important as strength.

For four months, he was unable to wear shoes. When he eventually could, they were at least a size too big so as not to damage his recovering toes.

Shockingly, a mere seven months after the amputation, Gardner was wrestling again. At first, he was tentative, sluggish, and, not surprisingly, a bit uncoordinated. He lost some matches he previously would have won.

But he also showed the old Rulon in spurts. His coaches were encouraged that Gardner's second miracle on the mat would come to fruition and he would work his way into contention for a berth on the U.S. squad for the Athens Games.

"This is all just preparation now," Fraser said in early 2003, a year after that frozen night. "He's going to improve a lot more with his feet, with his conditioning and with his timing. I'm fired up. I think he's not only going to come back the way he was, but better."

A tall order, of course. And one that Rulon Gardner already had shown was very much possible.

There were setbacks. He fell during a match at the national championships, and when he lost to a former training partner, he finished third at the event. Extremely impressive for most everyone, but disappointing in Gardner's mind.

Required to get down to 264 pounds to meet the new weight limit in his division, Gardner was forced to alter his wrestling style and still stay strong and in competitive shape.

Big deal. Gardner soon was winning big matches again. He defeated 2002 world champion Dremiel Byers to get back onto the U.S. team for the 2003 worlds in Paris; Gardner had won the world crown in 2001.

"No matter how far I go," he said, "I feel I succeeded just by making the team this year."

So his 10th-place finish at worlds wasn't distressing. Gardner estimated he was back to 99 percent of what he was in Sydney.

"I don't think I will ever get that 1 percent back," he admitted. "But you adjust. It's like people who are blind hear better. I am in better shape, quicker, more focused. I'm a better wrestler than I was before."

To truly prove that to the rest of the world, if not to himself, Gardner knew he had to make a strong run at the 2004 Olympic squad. The biggest hurdles, he figured, would be Byers and Cory Farkas, who beat Gardner at the 2003 nationals.

But then Gardner was in a motorcycle accident. He was thrown from his bike after a collision with a car, and while his injuries were minor, they were the last things he needed while training for a shot at the Olympic team.

Weeks later, he dislocated his right wrist playing basketball.

At the national championships, Byers defeated Gardner, who barely could use his right arm.

He also knew that when he reached the Olympic trials in May, anything short of making the squad would send him into retirement. He wasn't ready for that.

"It's my last hurrah if I don't win," he noted with a shrug. "If I do, I'm looking at Athens. Or else retirement. This will be the final chapter if I lose."

He didn't lose early in the trials, and when he pinned Farkas and blanked Paul Devlin 5-0, he was in the best-of-three finals against Byers.

"Here's two world champions going at it, putting it on the line on one mat," Gardner said. "I have three more matches to make the Olympic team. It's all I could ask for."

But could anyone really ask for anything more from this man, this champion? Had Gardner fallen to Byers, he still would have been an American hero, owner of the biggest upset victory in his sport's history.

Then again, could anything really stop Gardner at this point? After what he'd been through since dethroning Karelin, no challenge was daunting.

In their first match of the final round, Byers and Gardner went to overtime. Each time Byers got aggressive, Gardner had the answer. He frustrated Byers's every move and won 2-1.

Gardner's experience paid off in the next match, as well. Byers simply couldn't find anything that Gardner hadn't seen and countered. Again, they went to overtime. Again, Gardner won 2-1.

Hello, Athens!

"For me to get back to the Games was a whole battle in itself," he said. "For me to get there, a dream came true again."

There was a huge difference in Athens, though. Gardner knew that, win or lose, he would be leaving his shoes on the mat after his final match. He would leave competitive wrestling after these Olympics.

With Karelin no longer a factor—and despite the tribulations of the past two and a half years—Gardner was considered a medal favorite in Greece.

And he did get to the medal round, albeit not for the gold. An early loss to a Kazak wrestler—oddly, Gardner struggled in the clinches that were his strength against Karelin—relegated him to a bout for the bronze against Iran's Sajad Barzi.

While his 3-0 decision over Barzi hardly approached the drama of Sydney, Gardner's emotions ran wild at the conclusion of the match. With tears in his eyes—and in the eyes of many observers in the hall—he sat down, with an American flag in his arms, removed his shoes, and, as tradition demands, placed them on the mat.

Bawling like a baby, Gardner circled the arena with the flag, the cheers growing louder with every step.

To many, he'd pulled off yet another miracle. And two miracles in one lifetime was more than enough for Gardner.

"I came back and won a medal," he said. "It's a bronze medal, and I have no regrets, because I gave it 100 percent on the mat, every match. I didn't leave anything on the mat."

Oh yes he did. Gardner left his shoes—and a wonderful legacy.

# 8

## UPSET BY UPSET

As sports shockers go, no athlete who's pulled off a stunning upset has been more appropriately named than, well, Upset.

And no victim has been more accomplished than Man o' War.

By the middle of his two-year-old racing campaign in 1919, Man o' War was approaching legendary status among horse racing fans. He was the epitome of the word *thoroughbred*, an animal with no weaknesses, even at such a tender age.

Indeed, stable owners, trainers, jockeys, exercise riders, sports writers—nearly everyone involved with the sport—already had declared Man o' War among the greatest four-legged creatures the Sport of Kings had ever seen.

And he was just getting started when he headed to Saratoga, then the Taj Mahal of the thoroughbreds.

And when Man o' War won the United States Hotel Stakes

for his sixth consecutive triumph, he was being declared unbeatable.

Defeat was so unthinkable that Big Red, as he was affectionately being called in racing circles, probably could have been standing sideways when the Sanford Memorial began and still run away from the competition.

Well, not quite.

In those days, well before electronic starting gates, horses were lined up behind a mesh tape that was dropped by the track's starter.

On this day, August 13, the regular starter was absent, and the substitute was, well, not in the class of the horses lined up.

It was a pretty good group challenging Big Red, too. In the field was Golden Broom, who was owned by the niece of Sam Riddle, Man o' War's owner, and considered among the elite two-year-olds of the nation.

Indeed, before either horse had been entered in a race, Golden Broom outran Man o' War in a trial race back on the farm.

And there was Upset, who hardly seemed a candidate to pull one off and had already lost to Man o' War.

According to Upset's jockey, Willie Knapp, his steed was far inferior to Man o' War—and Upset carried 15 fewer pounds.

"If there is one horse that should've retired undefeated, Big Red was the one," Knapp said years later. "I never saw one like him and we never will again."

Man o' War tended to act up before the start of races, mainly because of his eagerness to run. In training long before getting to the track, Man o' War was nearly untamed. He fought off any sort of restraints, and not because he was ornery. He simply wanted to sprint.

His trainer, Louis Feustel, called Big Red "a fractious cuss."

"The first time I put a saddle on Big Red, he bucked and

sun-danced like a bronco," Feustel said. "He tossed his rider and ran around the paddock like a wild horse. Then he calmed down.

"You had to watch your step all the time."

Legend has it that with his regular jockey, Johnny Loftus, in the saddle for a workout, Big Red once reared back, nearly standing up straight on his hind legs. Then he took off down the track with Loftus hanging on for his life, running a half-mile in almost world-record time.

So beating Man o' War was not really on the minds of the jockeys and trainers and owners of the horses who opposed him.

"I think they knew when Red was on the track, they were racing for second," Feustel said.

Not on this hot August day in Saratoga.

When the assistant starter dropped the mesh, Man o' War was facing the wrong way and was flat-footed. The other entries responded well to the start. Big Red, already carrying high weight of 130 pounds, was in big trouble.

Loftus had to get Man o' War turned in the right direction before he could set off after the field. It took him a half-mile to catch up to the tailender in the race.

At that point, Loftus made a tactical blunder. He kept Man o' War on the rail, hoping to save ground as he reached the other contenders.

While that might have been the shortest route, it also was the most congested.

And for a reason. Knapp, aboard Upset, had decided that if he could trap the favorite on the inside, perhaps his horse or Golden Broom could steal the race.

Loftus found no holes near the rail, and in the stretch he was forced to veer Big Red to the outside, costing him more lengths in the chase to the wire.

Golden Broom was in the lead, but he faded and Upset moved in front.

In the final strides—and Man o' War took huge strides that some said were three or four feet *longer* than other thoroughbreds—Upset seemed doomed.

But it was too much to ask of Man o' War, or probably any horse. He'd spotted the field too big a lead, and while Upset won by a tiny margin, it was just enough.

"Another two strides and we would have won," Loftus said.

In essence, Man o' War had run perhaps a furlong more than the rest of the field. For years, observers would debate whether the race was fixed, or if the manner in which the other jockeys tag-teamed Big Red was fair.

To understand just how huge an upset 100-to-1 Upset had pulled off, it's necessary to examine the rest of Man o' War's brilliant career, which ended in 1920—yet nearly 80 years later got Big Red voted the best thoroughbred of the 20th century.

"He was a horse that had more of everything than any other horse," race historian B. K. Beckwith once told the *Los Angeles Times*. "He had more speed and stamina, and he looked the part of a champion. It all fit together. He started as a great horse. You couldn't beat him. He was a great big chestnut who ran like a flame."

Not only would Man o' War never lose another race, finishing with 20 victories in 21 starts, but only once would he be remotely challenged.

The remainder of his two-year-old campaign might have seemed like a lesson in how to avenge defeat, but that's far too simplistic an observation. Ten days after that loss, Man o' War was "the Man" again, romping in the Grand Union Hotel Stakes, with Upset well in arrears.

He also won the Futurity, the biggest race for juveniles, further stamping his greatness.

By then, Big Red was a big draw, too. The entire industry was benefiting from his popularity, with tracks across the country reporting big turnouts. On days when Man o' War raced, the grandstands usually were packed.

Riddle found his horse in such demand that he was fielding six-digit offers for the colt. His response often was, "Not in a million years for a million dollars."

Riddle decided to delay Man o' War's debut as a three-year-old. The owner was certain that the Kentucky Derby on the first Saturday in May was too early for a horse to peak. The one-and-a-quarter-mile Derby was not the all-encompassing event it soon would become, and it had to make do without Man o' War, as a colt named Paul Jones won the roses.

But the Preakness at Pimlico was another story. Riddle's farm was in Berlin, Maryland, so he knew Big Red would have a tremendous following in Baltimore. There also was some intrigue because Loftus had his license to ride suspended, and Clarence Kummer would be aboard the horse.

Plus, Upset was in the field.

Another chance for a surprise? No way.

Although Man o' War didn't show the scintillating burst for which he'd become famous, he never was in danger of failing. He even eased up down the stretch under Kummer, who felt it wise to save some of Big Red's energy.

"In that kind of company," Kummer said, "once we got in front, we weren't going to be headed."

Having put Upset in his place twice, Man o' War broke the world record in the Withers Stakes, even though he barely broke a sweat.

Then came the Belmont, but there were almost no takers. Only one horse, Donnacona, was entered, and the race was over as soon as it started.

The 1920 Belmont hardly was a classic, with Big Red winning by 20 lengths. But his time, a world record of 2:15 ⅕ that would stand for 46 years, was memorable.

Man o' War won that race at 1-to-100 odds; there even was a gambler who won $1,000 on the race by betting $100,000.

By then, handicappers were placing as much weight as possible on Man o' War in a vain attempt to even the field. He was faced with walkovers when other trainers would not put their horses on the track against him. In the Lawrence Realization, when every entry but one scratched rather than face Big Red, he won by 100 lengths. He carried an absurd 138 pounds in the Potomac Stakes and cruised to a six-length win.

The capper for Man o' War came in the Dwyer Stakes at Aqueduct late in the season. Big Red was a sports icon in the first year of the Roaring Twenties, but he'd actually oppose some quality horses in the Dwyer.

In particular, John P. Grier was in the field, his owners having methodically set out a schedule that would bring him into top shape for a race with Man o' War. John P. Grier would carry only 108 pounds to 126 for Man o' War.

"There were some at the racetrack that day who expected Red to be beaten," Kummer said. "I wasn't one of them, though."

Neither, presumably, was Man o' War, but for once he was challenged. In the most exciting race of his career, other than the loss to Upset, Man o' War was neck and neck with John P. Grier nearly the entire event. In the final yards, Big Red surged and won by one and a quarter lengths.

"It was a smashing race," racing historian Fred Van Ness told the *Los Angeles Times*. "A struggle between two really great horses.

"We saw Man o' War forced to run his best, his rider obliged to go to the whip in the stretch drive after the contestants had set such a dazzling pace from the very start that they seemed fairly to fly through space rather than touch the ground."

Man o' War followed that with a rout of Sir Barton in a match race. All Sir Barton had done in 1919 was become the first Triple Crown winner.

Sir Barton managed to come within 17 lengths—17 lengths!—at the wire.

A nation of racing fans eagerly anticipated the feats Big Red would accomplish as a four-year-old, but the only producing he would do after 1920 was at stud. Riddle was not going to subject Man o' War to carrying 140 pounds or more in handicap races, and he knew no track would give the great horse a break in weight.

Plus, Man o' War's career was pretty satisfying to say the least. He'd won $250,000, an unimaginable sum at the time. He was 20-for-21, and the only upset, to Upset, was, well, a fluke.

As another racing historian, Joe Palmer, once wrote in *American Race Horses*:

"He did not beat, he merely annihilated. He did not run to world records, he galloped to them. He was so far superior to his contemporaries that they could not extend him.

"He dominated racing as perhaps no athlete—not [tennis's Bill] Tilden or [golf's Bobby] Jones or [boxing's Jack] Dempsey or [Joe] Louis or [track's Paavo] Nurmi or [Jim] Thorpe or any human athlete—had dominated his sport."

# 9

## SHAKING DOWN THE THUNDER

It was long before the Notre Dame name was magic. Long before Knute Rockne became an American icon. Before his "win one for the Gipper" speech became part of the American language. And before the Four Horsemen were outlined against a blue-gray October sky.

And long, long before any college football program developed the mystique of the Fighting Irish, in large part thanks to Rockne and his "inspirational salesmanship."

In 1913, Rockne was just a student-athlete, a prematurely balding senior who played end. And Notre Dame was just a small Catholic school from the Midwest trying to put itself on America's football map.

Not much was known about the Notre Dame football team outside of the Midwest.

With one game against Army at West Point, that would change. And along with it, the sport of football would be altered—forever.

The Big Ten had unknowingly done Notre Dame a favor a few years earlier by blackballing the Irish. That probably was because the little Catholic school from South Bend, Indiana, had given the larger, proud Big Ten teams more than they could handle over the years.

Shut out by some of its natural rivals such as Michigan, Michigan State, Purdue, and Indiana, Notre Dame was forced to go elsewhere for competition. In 1913, the schedule was flavored by such teams as Texas, Penn State, and Army—all road games.

"I was just looking for games," said newly appointed Notre Dame coach Jesse Harper, "so I sat down and wrote a few letters."

Harper's football experience had been well documented by the time he arrived on the Notre Dame campus in 1913. He had played for the legendary Amos Alonzo Stagg at Chicago University and coached at Wabash College in Indiana. He brought along some of Stagg's football philosophies—most important, the forward pass.

The pass had been legalized in 1906 following sweeping rule changes that made football a less dangerous game.

"They were using the forward pass [at Chicago University]," James Harper, Jesse Harper's son, said in an interview in the 1970s. "They had a football like a rugby ball today. When [Dad] passed the ball, he couldn't grip it. It would just lay in his hand and he'd throw it. And he was a very accurate passer with it, but they didn't pass more than 35 yards. None of these 60–70 yard passes like today."

Actually, Jesse Harper wasn't actively seeking a job when Notre Dame came calling at Wabash.

"Dad was talking to an attorney who was a Notre Dame graduate," James Harper recalled. "Dad made the comment that football should be made to pay for itself. In those days, none of the sports paid for themselves. This attorney conveyed that comment to the president of Notre Dame, and he said, 'I want to see that man.' That was how Dad got hired by Notre Dame."

Football wasn't the only sport Jesse Harper coached at Wabash; he also coached baseball and track.

"In those days, you did everything," James Harper said.

At Notre Dame, Jesse Harper fell into a good situation. The Irish already had a solid football program in place.

From 1906–1912, the Irish boasted four unbeaten seasons and a record of 44-3-5. In 1912, the second straight undefeated season under John L. Marks, Notre Dame had pounded opponents by scores such as 116-7, 74-7, and 69-0.

By that time, Rockne had become one of the stars of the squad, along with quarterback Gus Dorais.

Rockne had come a long way following a slow start in 1910. In his first try at football, Rockne was sent out with the scrubs by Notre Dame coach Frank "Shorty" Longman in a test against the regulars. Rockne was nervous and scared.

"He made me a fullback," remembered Rockne. "They should have changed my position to drawback."

Never was a freshman so shaken.

"Trying to spear my first punt I had frozen fingers and the ball rolled everywhere it wasn't wanted."

Rockne recalled that Longman pulled him off the field.

"I was a washout," Rockne recalled, "not even good enough for the scrubs."

But there was nothing wrong with Rockne's legs. The 145-pounder could outrace the wind. He made the Notre Dame track team and eventually earned a spot for himself as an end on the football varsity. By then, his pass-catching skills had improved considerably.

"I had the pleasant surprise of seeing myself discussed as an All-America possibility toward the end of the 1912 season," Rockne later recalled.

The Irish had another All-American prospect in Dorais, a 5-foot-7, 145-pound quarterback who could pass, run, and kick with equal efficiency.

Rockne took an immediate liking to his new teammate, probably because he saw a lot of himself in Dorais.

"Like myself," Rockne said, "Gus had to fight for everything he got. Neither of us was very big, and the fellow with the small build has to be so much more clever to hold his own against the bigger boys."

When Dorais came out for football as a freshman in 1910, it was customary for the Notre Dame players to warm up for practice by kicking the ball. Not Dorais. He threw the ball instead—gripping the pigskin at the end and using the same overhand motion he used as a pitcher in baseball.

"You throw the ball pretty well," Notre Dame coach Longman told Dorais, "but you don't hold it right. You'll never be able to handle a wet ball like that. It'll slip out of your hand."

Longman felt that Dorais would do better by holding the ball flat and sailing it underhand, the other prevailing style of the day.

The cocky Dorais thought Longman was wrong. The ball was soaked in a bucket of water, and Dorais proved his point by firing a pass without a hitch.

When Harper took over as the Notre Dame coach in 1913, he looked over the far-reaching schedule and knew it wasn't going to be easy.

Before his players went home for the summer, Harper gave a football to Dorais and Rockne and told them to throw it around whenever they had any leisure time.

The two of them took the suggestion from Harper to heart, practicing daily at a beach resort in Cedar Point, Ohio.

"I'd run along the beach, Dorais would throw from all angles," Rockne once recalled. "People who didn't know we were two college seniors making painstaking preparations for our final season probably thought we were crazy."

It didn't stop the pair from what Rockne called "daily, tedious practice."

"Rockne continued to develop his deceptive, stop-and-go style of going down the field for a pass, a style used by all good pass receivers," Dorais pointed out. "I worked hard to increase the accuracy and length of my passes."

When they came back to school in the fall of 1913, Dorais and Rockne were eager to put their keenly developed skills to the test. They were especially looking forward to the Army game on November 1, as were the rest of the Fighting Irish.

The November 1 contest, fourth on the schedule, had been hastily arranged by the schools. For the Fighting Irish, it was a way of getting national attention. For the Cadets, it was a way to fill an open date on the schedule—albeit against a "mystery team" like Notre Dame.

"I was in the Cadet locker room on a Thursday afternoon following practice when I first heard of the Indiana institution called Notre Dame," said Willet J. Baird, the Army mascot. "The players, as usual, were asking questions about this Indiana team and no one present seemed to know a great deal about it."

Most everyone, however, was convinced that Saturday's game would be a "breather."

Why not? Army, which had started the year 4-0 by outscoring the opposition 72-6, had a bigger reputation and a far bigger team than Notre Dame. The Cadets outweighed the Irish by 10 to 15 pounds to the man.

The Cadets played in the elite East. Their competition usually included Harvard, Princeton, and Yale, the Big Three of the Ivy League who were perennially in contention for the national championship. And Army usually held its own against these teams.

At that time, eastern football was considered the class of the country. And the Ivy League was the class of the East.

Notre Dame also had the disadvantage of playing on Army's home field following a long and arduous train trip from the Midwest.

First there was a dreary all-day trip to Buffalo. Then the Notre Dame players changed trains and boarded a "sleeper." They arrived at West Point after an overnight trip, looking much the worse for wear.

The 18 players carried their own uniforms in satchels, and some wore their jerseys under their coats to conserve space on this spartan journey. The only extra equipment was a roll of tape, a jar of liniment, and a bottle of iodine.

"They came without the usual large trunks which were carried in those days by many leading eastern teams," pointed out Baird. "They presented the usual appearance of a small college team which considered itself lucky to have so many players."

The wide-eyed Notre Dame players were impressed with the West Point campus, particularly Cullum Hall Field, where Army played its games.

"Most of the players visiting the playing field expressed no end of amazement and joy over the fact that the field was very smooth, well-marked and resembled the appearance of a well-kept lawn," Baird said.

Notre Dame had received $1,000 in expenses from Army to transport its players and coach. Apparently, it was not enough to outfit the whole team.

While dressing in the locker room on game day, the Notre

Dame players asked the Army equipment manager if he could spare two extra pairs of football pants. And some ankle wraps, knee guards, supporters, extra shoe strings, and several pairs of shoes.

The Irish were not only underdogs but also ill-equipped underdogs.

Then it was game time. Rockne, the Notre Dame captain, shook hands with Army captain Benny Hogue at midfield. Notre Dame won the coin toss and elected to receive—a bad idea, it seemed, when Dorais fumbled the ball and Army recovered on the Irish 27.

But Notre Dame held on downs, despite taking a terrific pounding from the heavier Army line.

Notre Dame ball.

Convention dictated a plunge or two by the Notre Dame backs. As the first play unfolded, the Cadets sent their guards and tackles crashing into the middle of the Notre Dame line to stop the expected run.

Surprise!

Dorais neatly stepped back and flicked the ball to a receiver for an 11-yard gain and a first down.

Then another aerial surprise. And still another.

The Irish gained three quick first downs with their passing against the bewildered Cadets.

At first Dorais's main target was halfback Joe Pliska. Then it was Rockne's turn.

With his speed, he had left an Army defensive back flatfooted on one play as he raced toward the goal line.

"Dorais whipped the ball and the grandstands roared at the completion of the 40-yard pass," Rockne recalled. "Everybody seemed astonished. There had been no hurdling, no tackling, no plunging, no crushing of fiber and sinew. Just a long-distance touchdown by rapid transit."

Though stunned by Notre Dame's passing game, the Cadets managed to stay within a point in the first half, 14-13.

In the second half, the Cadets made some adjustments by keeping their defenders wide. What did Dorais do? He simply sent fullback Ray Eichenlaub inside for a pair of rushing TDs. When Army then changed its tactic to stop the Notre Dame running game, Dorais took to the air again for another touchdown.

The shocking final: Notre Dame 35, Army 13.

Dorais had thrown an unheard-of 17 passes, completing 14. By comparison with today's game, it doesn't sound like a lot. But back then, it was more than anyone could imagine. Certainly anyone in the East, the stronghold of college football at the time.

"Notre Dame's long forward passing and pretty open-field play was spectacular and a revelation to Eastern football enthusiasts," wrote the *Boston Globe*.

Notre Dame did not invent the forward pass. But the Fighting Irish certainly brought it to the nation's attention with their victory over Army that day. Notre Dame had shown everyone the possibilities. Football would never be the same again.

# 10

## DOWNING DIXIE

It was the upstart vs. the legend.

Young Don Haskins vs. the legendary Baron of the Bluegrass, Adolph Rupp.

The unknown vs. a basketball giant.

The Texas Western Miners, barely on the basketball map, vs. the four-time NCAA champion Kentucky Wildcats.

And black vs. white.

Texas Western played black men exclusively against all-white Kentucky. Rupp, known for his racial attitudes, would recruit only whites.

It was the first time in the history of the NCAA Division I finals that a team started five black players.

It was a landmark game with far-reaching social implications, although few people thought it at the time.

"Hell, I just played the best guys we had," Haskins said of his Texas Western team in 1966. "It didn't matter if they were black, white or whatever."

Haskins had always been color blind when it came to recruiting basketball players for Texas Western (long since renamed Texas El Paso, or UTEP).

Nolan Richardson, who would become a championship coach at Arkansas, played three years for Haskins. As did Jim "Bad News" Barnes, another black player who helped the Miners make the NCAA playoffs in 1963 and 1964.

In the 1966 finals, Kentucky was ranked No. 1 in the nation and was a heavy favorite to beat No. 3 Texas Western. Although each team came into the finals with only one loss, it was generally thought Kentucky played a stronger schedule.

Kentucky was one of the storied programs in college basketball. Under Rupp, the Wildcats won a string of Southeastern Conference titles and were usually the team to beat in that league every season. Rupp's teams often produced All-Americans and NBA prospects.

From 1948–1951, Kentucky basketball was at its zenith. The Wildcats won three national championships in four years, featuring such greats as Alex Groza, Wallace "Wah Wah" Jones, Cliff Barker, Ralph Beard, and Kenneth Rollins—the so-called Fabulous Five. These same players also helped the United States win the Olympic gold medal at the 1948 Games. The overall record compiled by the Fab Five at Kentucky: 125-12.

There were no Fab Five types on the 1958 team. Rupp called this bunch "the Fiddlin' Five" because "they fiddled around enough to drive me crazy." This team nevertheless won a fourth national title for Rupp.

"They weren't the greatest basketball players in the world," Rupp would say later. "All they could do was win."

By comparison with the earlier teams, the 1965–1966 Kentucky squad fell short—literally. The Wildcats of that year were the shortest Rupp had ever coached, with no starter taller than

6-foot-5. However, this lack of height did not stop the Wildcats from rising to the No. 1 ranking in the country.

Another team, another colorful appellation: Rupp's Runts.

The Runts, a straight-shooting, high-scoring bunch who averaged 88 points a game, were said to be Rupp's favorite team.

Rupp made the cover of *Sports Illustrated*, and his players made the pages of *Time* magazine. Wearing their letterman jackets, the highly touted Wildcats were photographed strolling around the Kentucky campus. "It was the most exciting time of my life," said Pat Riley, who would go on to become a title-winning coach in the NBA.

Rupp, a Kansas native who had a highly superstitious nature, favored wearing brown suits; he had a closet full of them. Often called "the Man in the Brown Suit," Rupp would wear the same outfit until the Wildcats lost a game. Then he would switch to another brown suit.

There was quite a bit of suit changing in the 1964–1965 season, when the Wildcats won only 15 of 25 games, Rupp's worst year.

In 1965–1966, the Kentucky coach didn't have to give much thought to his clothes. The Wildcats put together a superb 26-1 record heading into the Final Four.

The Runts had a strong mix of quickness and power with seniors (Larry Conley and Tommy Kron), juniors (Riley and Louie Dampier), and sophomore center Thad Jaracz. Kentucky's weakest position was thought to be at center, but when Jaracz scored 32 points in a key intersectional victory over Illinois, the Wildcats had erased any doubts about a weakness in their starting lineup.

Meanwhile, no one gave Texas Western much chance to contend for the national championship. Who—or what—was Texas Western? El Paso, Texas, was well known, but not for basketball. It was the gateway to Juarez, Mexico, and it was the locale for a famous country music song.

The Miners didn't have one player who made an all-district team in high school. One coach told Haskins he could never win a championship with an all-black lineup. The misguided conventional thinking then: "They don't do well under pressure."

One day, Haskins invited his team captain, Harry Flournoy, into his office.

"He asked me what I thought he should do," Flournoy said many years later. "I was just a kid. He was the coach, and I thought they knew everything. Finally, I said, 'Coach, I think you just ought to put your best players on the floor.'"

Haskins, a big bear of a man in his sixth year of coaching at Texas Western, wasn't thinking about racial crusading. In his words, he was just "a punk trying to win a few basketball games."

And his team did win. The Miners started out as one of the hottest teams in America, knocking off their first nine opponents.

Still, Haskins was troubled. The opponents were relatively weak, and Haskins thought he detected some complacency in his team.

"I don't know if it's that easy to coach a great team," Haskins said. "They get to know how great they are, and they won't listen to you. These guys could guard people like nobody I ever saw, but they 'bout drove me crazy because they played down all the time."

"These guys" included the top seven of Dave "Big Daddy" Lattin, Bobby Joe Hill, Willie Cager, Orsten Artis, Nevil Shed, Willie Worsley, and Flournoy—most from urban areas. Cager, Shed, and Worsley were products of New York City. Hill came from Detroit, and Lattin from Houston. Artis and Flournoy were discovered in basketball-rich Gary, Indiana.

None of their opponents seemed to notice the first seven players on the Texas Western team were black. Many teams on the Miners' schedule featured black players in the lineup themselves.

This was not true all across America, of course, particularly in the South. It was a different America then. Despite a law that racial segregation in schools was unconstitutional, leagues such as the Atlantic Coast Conference, the Southwestern Conference, and Kentucky's own Southeastern Conference refused to recruit black players. They had drawn a line—in this case, at the Mason-Dixon Line. This even included playing against teams with blacks in the lineup. In the early 1960s, an SEC team refused an invitation to the NCAA playoffs because it had a policy of not playing against integrated teams.

When Rupp was ordered by the school president to recruit black players, he made a token visit to one home. He made it undeniably clear to the family that he wasn't happy about being there. Needless to say, the player went elsewhere.

As the 1960s roared on with its dramatic cultural changes and social revolutions, sports was every bit a part of it. In the 1963 NCAA tournament, George Ireland's Loyola of Chicago team featured four blacks in its starting lineup.

After a victory over Tennessee Tech in the first round, the Loyola Ramblers were scheduled to face Mississippi State in Round 2. That was not agreeable with Mississippi governor Ross R. Barnett, who banned the team from participating in the tourney.

Mississippi State practiced racial segregation and didn't normally play against schools with black players. But this time, diverting state police with a decoy team, Mississippi State players managed to scramble out of town and travel to the tournament for their meeting with Loyola.

In the end, they probably wished they hadn't after losing 61-51 to the eventual national champion.

Three years later, Texas Western would make history when it started five black players in the NCAA finals.

Haskins's Miners played a rugged defense and disciplined offense, a style he had learned 15 years earlier under Hall of Fame coach Hank Iba.

In the 1966 NCAA tournament, the Miners knocked off such powerhouses as Cincinnati, Kansas, and Utah to set up a meeting with Kentucky in the finals.

Flournoy, a ferocious rebounder, was the key for Texas Western in a one-point double-overtime victory over Kansas in the Midwest Regional. The 6-foot-5 Flournoy blocked a dunk attempt by 6-11 All-American Walt Wesley, preserving the thrilling victory.

Observers, meanwhile, were paying more attention to Kentucky after the Wildcats had beaten Michigan in an earlier round and then took second-ranked Duke in the national semifinals. That game, everyone thought, would actually decide the national championship.

The Wildcats had rolled into College Park, Maryland, a pretty sick bunch despite their playoff successes. Rupp complained that many of his players suffered illnesses of one kind or another while competing in the Mideast Regional in Iowa City. Rupp was most concerned about Conley, his key player, who complained of chest pains, a bad throat, and fever.

"I'm taking a bunch of sick boys to the championship finals," Rupp said.

Still, Kentucky was the strong favorite among the betting crowd to whip this "no-name" school in the finals.

The Miners were treated with a lack of respect in other ways, particularly by Rupp. At a pregame press conference, Rupp unkindly repeated a rumor that some of Texas Western's players had been in jail. Hot Rod Hundley, the West Virginia star, said the Miners could do everything with a basketball "except sign it." (Actually, not one of the Texas Western players had been to prison, nor ever would be. And 9 of the 12 players on the team would graduate, a higher percentage than Kentucky's players.) The highly focused Miners remained stoically detached from the media circus that Rupp created with his comments.

"If we were thinking, 'We've got to beat these whiteys,' it might have affected us," Shed said in an interview 30 years later. "But we never thought that way."

Even though the Miners went into the championship game as the underdog, Haskins and his players didn't feel that way.

"I played for the best coach who ever lived: Henry Iba," Haskins said. "I wasn't intimidated by Adolph Rupp."

Before the game, Haskins repeated to his players Rupp's declaration that "no five blacks are going to beat Kentucky." But how to match up against Kentucky's quickness, power, and scoring?

To counteract Kentucky's speed, Haskins introduced a three-guard lineup featuring Hill, Artis, and Worsley. Hill and Artis were the Miners' regular backcourt duo, while Worsley replaced the bigger Shed. And Haskins implored his players to pick up their defense.

For weeks leading up to the finals, Haskins was unhappy with the defensive play of his Miners—and he let them know about it in tough practices.

Haskins was relentless and merciless, holding three-and-a-half-hour practice sessions without allowing his players a single drink of water. His players ran sprints until they were exhausted, and then some.

"The coach had a way of making you work harder than you really wanted to," remembered Shed.

"He'd say, 'You big girl, it's time to put a skirt on you. If your brains were dynamite, you'd blow up the whole gym.' Then he'd make us run up the stairs again."

Haskins was sure the Miners could play better defense than they had in earlier games. In fact, they had to if they wanted to beat Kentucky.

Haskins also wanted to make a statement on offense against the shorter Kentucky team. Midway through the first half, Lattin did so with a two-hand dunk shot over Riley.

That made it 16-11 Texas Western and set the stage for more to come. There was also this surprise: an exquisite defense led by the peppery Hill.

First he stole the ball from Kron, dribbled half the court, and scored on an easy layup. Then he took the ball away from Dampier and went in for another easy shot.

Texas Western led 31-28 at the half, and the Miners came out in the second half with more determination. Hill converted seven more steals into baskets after intermission.

The Miners' skintight defense forced the Wildcats into one low percentage shot after another, and Kentucky spent the rest of the game trying to catch up. The Wildcats couldn't.

At the final buzzer, Texas Western was a shocking 72-65 winner. One Wildcats player said it wasn't as close as the score indicated.

As the youthful coach of the Texas Western basketball team, Haskins had just accomplished the improbable—some said the impossible.

"It was a thrill playing against Mr. Rupp, let alone beating him," Haskins said.

Then the racists came out in droves.

"We filled up trash baskets with those letters," said Haskins, who claimed he read every one. "People from all over were calling my players names that started with the little letter 'n.' White people were saying I used them to win games. Black people said I had exploited the players."

Few knew it at the time, but an era was ending in college basketball. Texas Western's victory was generally credited with opening doors at universities around the country for black basketball players. It had a far-reaching effect not only on sports but on American society as well. Even schools in the South soon had to change their old-line way of thinking.

Three years after the landmark game in College Park, Kentucky signed its first black player. Seven years after the finals at College Park, Alabama had an all-black lineup.

By the time Haskins retired in 1999, he had coached 38 Miners teams, gone to the NCAA playoffs 14 times, and won 719 games.

It's obvious which team brought him the most satisfaction.

"When I look at teams like the University of Texas and see that it's no big deal to have a black player any more, that makes me feel good," said Haskins, who was inducted into the Naismith Basketball Hall of Fame in 1997.

# 11

## BILLY MILLS, THE LAKOTA LEGEND

As Billy Mills toed the starting line for the 10,000-meter race at the 1964 Tokyo Olympics, he couldn't help but glance at the people next to him. Did he really belong with the likes of Ron Clarke, the world's best distance runner; Mohamed Gammoudi; Mamo Wolde; Pyotr Bolotnikov, who won the 10,000 at the 1960 Rome Games; and defending Olympic 5,000 champion Murray Halberg?

Or even with Gerry Lindberg, his teammate who had beaten Mills at the Olympic trials?

Actually, self-doubt had become too much of a companion for Mills, who'd quit running competitively in 1962 after starring at the University of Kansas and establishing himself as one of the best Native American long-distance competitors ever.

"I felt I should have been doing better, that I had the talent, but I wasn't using it the best I could," said Mills, a lieutenant in the Marines during much of his racing career, stationed at Camp Pendelton, California. "I was pretty much disgusted."

His wife, Pat, convinced Mills that he was wasting a magnificent opportunity, that his skills were special. He simply needed to channel them correctly.

The retirement didn't last long—18 months. Soon, the love for running returned.

"You follow the body, mind and spirit; it doesn't allow you to quit," he said. "Running became my passion, the Olympics my dream."

Long before Mills could cash in on that dream, he'd experienced the worst aspects of American society. A member of the Oglala Lakota Sioux nation, he was often confronted with a double dose of racism because he was also part white. There were instances when he wasn't allowed to compete, or opponents ganged up on the young Mills to make sure he didn't beat them.

Mills easily could have turned away from the sport, turned away from seeking goals, turned away from building something memorable.

"That's where the dreams lie. You've got to dig so deep through all those emotions to find the dreams," he said. "You get to know yourself. You find the passion. You're self-motivated."

Mills always needed to be self-motivated. Born in South Dakota, where he grew up on a reservation that was racked by poverty, he was an orphan by age 12—along with seven siblings. He wound up in a boarding school run by the U.S. government before attending a high school for Native Americans, the Haskell Institute in Lawrence, Kansas.

At Haskell, he began his running career. He also was inspired by a deep pride in his heritage and remained so after earning a scholarship to Kansas, then among the most accomplished track programs in the country.

And also one of the most biased campuses during that era.

"I've traveled to 85 different countries, but when I went to the University of Kansas, I experienced more cultural shock than in any of those places," Mills said years after his running career ended. "Of course, it was not the University of Kansas that was the problem. It was America.

"As a student at KU, I was in conflict, half Indian and half white. The Indian world rejected me as mixed blood. The white world accepted me as an athlete but rejected me as a friend. I was challenged to live my life as a warrior."

As a result of the social pressures, Mills's life took on a deeply philosophical fervor. He carries on his personal crusade today.

"I want to challenge you to seek unity in your soul, to seek unity in your spirit, . . . and to seek unity in America through cultural diversity."

Mills has devoted his life to those goals, but he likely never would have earned the platform to make a difference had he not been standing in the Olympic Stadium in Tokyo on October 14, 1964.

The previous day, the unheralded Mills purchased a new pair of track shoes in the Olympic Village. At the same time, shoe manufacturers were handing out free samples to Clarke and the other standouts of the day. They didn't even make an offer to Mills.

Mills hadn't even been interviewed in the week leading up to the race.

As if that wasn't enough of an insult, when Clarke was asked about others in the field, he never mentioned Mills. Indeed, when asked about facing Mills, he said, "Worry about him? I never heard of him."

Considering that Mills had failed to make the 1960 U.S. team, he had stopped running for one and a half years, and his best time was nearly a minute slower than the world record for the 10,000, why should the Australian have been concerned about the American?

Clarke's strategy was to surge at various points in the first half of the event, hoping to leave the others so far behind that their competitive spirit would be broken. By 5,000 meters, his plan had worked on all but Ethiopia's Wolde; Tunisia's Gammoudi; Japan's Kokichi Tsuburaya, who responded magnificently to the cheers of his countrymen; and Mills.

Mills? He was on pace to break 28 minutes and 30 seconds, territory he'd never even approached.

But on the 20th of 24 laps, Mills faded. He almost lost contact with Clarke—who now was setting a grueling pace—Gammoudi, and Wolde. Mills was through.

Or was he? Suddenly, he began to sprint, and by the end of the 21st lap, he had closed in on the group of leaders. By the 23rd lap, Wolde fell back to make it a three-man race.

As the final lap began, Clarke seemed stunned to have not only two runners right with him but also two men who never had posted career bests close to his. The favorite seemed to panic a bit when he couldn't shake them, and he shoved Mills toward the outside of the track in order to attempt a pass.

But that gave Gammoudi a huge opening, which he seized. Bumping both Clarke and Mills, he moved through them into the lead as the crowd roared in anticipation of a scintillating finish.

They got it. Clarke rallied back and was even with Gammoudi at the beginning of the final stretch. As those two staged a battle of wills and stamina, they forgot about Mills, who'd remained toward the outside lanes behind them.

With 100 meters to go, Mills began a desperate sprint. Neither the Australian nor the Tunisian ever sensed that Mills was a threat, but 50 meters from the line, Mills ran past both.

Neither Clarke nor Gammoudi had another burst left, and

Billy Mills, the longest of long shots at the Tokyo Games, broke the tape with a three-yard margin on Gammoudi. Clarke was third.

His time: 28:24.4, an Olympic record and 46 seconds faster than he'd ever covered 10,000 meters.

"This moment in time for me was God-given. I didn't

Getty Images

*Billy Mills catches his breath after winning the*
*10,000 meters at the 1964 Olympics.*

achieve it. I did all the work for it but it was God-given," Mills said. "That's the most humbling experience you can ever encounter."

Mills insisted it was more than just talent that drove him to the finish line. It was desire and faith.

"I realized, 'Wow, I didn't [only] win this race.' I found the passion. I pursued it with all the intensity possible, but with a vision and a mission statement that was value-based, and I kept it sacred."

Now the media knew who Mills was. He was surrounded by interviewers. He was lauded on American television, where his name barely was mentioned before the 10,000.

"I guess there weren't too many people in that stadium who believed I could win, other than me," he said. But now he was an American hero. A Native American hero.

He never got to take a victory lap because so many runners still were finishing the race. And, even though Marines supposedly don't cry, Mills shed tears on the victory stand. They weren't just tears of joy, for Mills understood his role as a Native American who had accomplished something unique.

He would use the voice such renown gave him to further the cause of equality in America. Mills, a track and field Hall of Famer, has campaigned for his people ever since that magical day in Tokyo.

Mills helped create Christian Relief Services, which has raised hundreds of millions of dollars for Native American youngsters and other charitable causes.

A youth center in Eagle Butte, South Dakota, is named after Mills, who helped arrange the funding for the facility in 1999 in his role as spokesman for Running Strong for American Indian Youth. He also represented the Native American Sports Council, which helps identify and fund potential Olympians from the American Indian community.

The 10,000 meters at the Kansas Relays also carries his name, as does a portion of a cross-country course in Kansas: the Billy Mills Ascent. He inspired the likes of Kevin Finley, the director of the athletic department at the United Tribes Technical College in Bismarck, North Dakota. Finley's school became a power in junior college basketball soon after he met with Mills.

"Billy never said a word to me about running," Finley said. "Rather, it was about having a goal and a plan. Beyond that, it was not to quit. I think a lot of what happened with United Tribes basketball was inspired by that.

"What he taught me was to fight through any obstacle, to break down barriers."

In 1988, a 17-year-old Native American named Chris Schurz became a top high school runner. He took up track in part because of the movie *Running Brave*, which starred Robby Benson as Billy Mills.

"He's almost like a saint," Schurz said after meeting Mills. "I can't believe how much he has given back to people. After I saw that movie, I always wanted to meet him. I always wanted to be like him."

Few sports upsets have had such a societal impact in America as Mills's run to glory.

"I quit my career at the age of 26, with the best eight years ahead of me," he said. "I'm not looked at in America as a great distance runner, but as a guy who came out of nowhere and created a big upset.

"What I took from sports," Mills proclaimed, "was the concept of global unity through the beauty, dignity and character of global diversity."

# 12

## RUINING THE BRUINS

*S*harpshooter *Phil Esposito has Ken Dryden in his sights.*

*The year: 1971. The Boston Bruins and Montreal Canadiens are playing the decisive seventh game of their Stanley Cup playoff series.*

*Esposito, who scored an NHL record 76 goals for the Bruins that season, is bearing down on the rookie Montreal goaltender, with the puck on his stick. He fires. A goal for sure.*

*But wait—Dryden stretches out the entire length of his body and deflects the puck before it crosses the goal line.*

*Esposito can't believe it. Neither can the hometown Boston crowd.*

*The Bruins center, who makes his living in front of the net, stares at Dryden and then curses him.*

*"He's a [bleeping] octopus!" he screams.*

*Esposito skates behind the net and slams his stick against the glass.*

Dryden's spectacular save wasn't anything new. He had been robbing the Bruins all series long.

And he would continue to do so as the Canadiens knocked the heavily favored Boston team out of the playoffs with a 4-2 win.

"Dryden was better than we had ever dreamed," said Boston star defenseman Bobby Orr.

Indeed. And who would have believed that a rookie goaltender starting his first playoff series could come in and mystify the Big, Bad Bruins?

The Bruins had run away with the East Division race, posting a 57-14-7 record for a league-best 121 points—24 more than the third-place Canadiens—and setting 37 team and individual NHL records.

Boston placed four players on the NHL First All-Star Team: Esposito at center, Orr on the blue line, Ken Hodge at right wing, and Johnny Bucyk at left wing.

The Bruins won the Stanley Cup in 1970 and were the odds-on favorites to win a second straight title and continue to build a dynasty.

A couple more things: The Bruins had beaten the Canadiens in five of their six regular-season meetings, scoring 13 of their 399 goals in two games in the final week of the season. Plus they had home-ice advantage in this first-round series.

They hadn't counted on a young goaltender untested in Stanley Cup play to throw a roadblock in front of them. Even though the lanky (6-foot-4) Dryden had starred at Cornell and played well on the Canadiens' farm team, no one expected him to be given the nod to start a playoff series.

True, Dryden looked sharp in six regular-season NHL games, but coaches usually like to go with experienced goalies in the playoffs. Imagine how surprised everyone was when coach Al MacNeil chose Dryden to start over Rogie Vachon, the Canadiens' top goalie, and his backup, Phil Myre.

Ironically, Dryden had been picked 14th overall in the 1964 amateur draft by the Bruins. But he decided to go to college instead of the NHL.

The Bruins eventually traded his rights to Montreal for Guy Allen and Paul Reid, two players who would never reach the NHL.

Sending Dryden in against Boston appeared downright suicidal. The Bruins were known not only for their scoring power but also as a tough, hard-hitting—some said dirty—team. Some clubs, such as the Canadiens, had historically won with finesse and skating ability. With their toughness and aggressive behavior, the Bruins brought a new dimension to the game. They set the standard for physical hockey that would be followed by the Philadelphia Flyers and others.

Orr, though, was a different kind of player. More flashy than physical, he revolutionized the game with wide-open play from his defensive position. Before Orr, defensemen generally stayed back to protect their own net and rarely joined in the offensive play. Orr changed all that. Taking the shackles off, Orr set a career scoring record for defensemen with 270 goals and 645 assists for 915 points. The record stood until broken many years later by Paul Coffey.

"I played a style that wasn't common," said Orr, who scored the Cup-winning goal in the Bruins' 4-3 overtime victory over St. Louis in 1970. "The thing about the way I played, the guys understood they would have to cover me left and right."

While the Canadiens boasted a First-Team All-Star in defenseman J. C. Tremblay and a second-teamer in right winger Yvon Cournoyer, they didn't match up with the legendary Canadiens teams of the past.

After expansion in 1967, Montreal won two straight Cups by beating the fledgling St. Louis Blues in the finals. But the mid- to late 1950s were the Canadiens' most awesome era. Featuring such greats as Maurice "Rocket" Richard; his brother, Henri; Jean Beliveau; Dickie Moore; Doug Harvey; Bernie "Boom Boom" Geoffrion; and goalie Jacques Plante—Hall of Famers all—the Canadiens won a record five straight Cups and six overall from 1951–1960.

The choice of Dryden for the Canadiens in the 1971 playoffs could have been easily second-guessed. The Bruins won the opener 3-1 as Orr scored a goal and assisted on another and Gerry Cheevers made 30 saves. There was probably even more second-guessing when the Bruins led 5-1 in the second period of the second game.

But Dryden got his game together—and so did his Montreal teammates. Led by the classy Beliveau, the Canadiens overcame the four-goal deficit and went on to a shocking 7-5 victory in Boston Garden.

Back in Montreal for Game 3, the Canadiens stopped the Bruins 3-1 with the help of two goals from veteran sharpshooter Frank Mahovlich, who joined the team in a midseason trade with Detroit. Dryden faced 37 shots, stopping all but one.

"Dryden, playing his third consecutive playoff game after only six regular-season NHL contests, was brilliant throughout the game," reported *United Press International*.

In Game 4, Orr showed why he was such a special player. The all-star defenseman scored three times to lead the Bruins to a 5-2 victory and tie the series at two games apiece.

Back in the cozy Boston Garden, where the Bruins had terrorized teams with their bloody, physical play, Montreal fell behind 5-1 through two periods.

In the third period, the Canadiens came out as if to duplicate their stunning comeback in Game 2 by scoring two quick

Getty Images

*The "octopus" who stymied the Boston Bruins during the 1971
Stanley Cup playoffs, Montreal Canadiens goalie Ken Dryden.*

goals. But the Bruins answered with two of their own late in
the game for a 7-3 victory to take a 3-2 lead in the series.

The Canadiens' defense obviously was not at its best in front
of Dryden, allowing the Bruins to take 54 shots. As it was, the
acrobatic Montreal goalie stopped 47 of them—a great night
under the circumstances and the pressure.

What could stop the Bruins now? They needed only one victory in the next two games to advance to the next round. And they had the safety net of a seventh game back in the Boston Garden.

So what happened? They were rocked by Montreal 8-3 in Game 6 as Henri Richard and Pete Mahovlich, Frank's younger brother, each scored twice. Dryden showed he could do more than just stop shots. He set up Mahovlich's second goal of the game with a pass along the boards.

What do you know, the Canadiens were still alive in the series. Now tied at three games apiece, the teams headed to the Boston Garden for a seventh-game showdown.

Dryden had proved to be a lifesaver for Montreal. In the first six games, he made some 250 saves against the high-powered Bruins.

As he and his Montreal teammates prepared for Game 7, Dryden was a little nervous. The night before the showdown, he had turned on the television in his hotel room. He wished he hadn't.

"The only thing I could find was 'The Bruins Week in Review,' or whatever it was called," Dryden said. "All they kept showing was the Bruins scoring goal after goal. Esposito scores! Orr scores! Esposito scores again! I was already nervous, and I turned downright depressed. I went to bed."

Following what Bruins coach Tom Johnson called the "worst game we've played all season," he hoped for better results in Game 7. Certainly the hometown atmosphere couldn't hurt. The Bruins didn't lose many important games at the Boston Garden.

On the Montreal side, John Ferguson probably spoke for all of his teammates when he said, "Stop Orr, and you *do* stop the Bruins."

Which is exactly what happened.

The Canadiens stuck to the Boston star like a magnet, allowing him only three shots the entire game. Once he even lost the puck to Jacques Lemaire, who passed to Frank Mahovlich for Montreal's third goal early in the third period.

"He was tireless through the whole series, but he looked tired about halfway through the game today," Dryden said of Orr. "And we gave him special attention."

Dryden, on the other hand, looked as if he was gaining strength with each miraculous save. The rookie stopped 46 of 48 shots in a pressure-packed game, allowing only a goal by Hodge in the first period and by Bucyk in the third. Most noticeably, Dryden stopped all 11 shots fired by the feared Esposito.

Meanwhile, Frank Mahovlich scored twice, and Rejean Houle and Tremblay each had a goal to help the Canadiens finish off the mighty Bruins by a 4-2 score.

After one tremendous save on a close-in shot by Esposito, Dryden noticed that the Boston players looked frustrated.

"I looked at the faces of the Bruins," Dryden would say later, "and I could see it all so clearly. They all looked defeated."

Defeated they were, mostly thanks to Dryden.

"Words cannot even describe the way Dryden played," Hodge said.

The Canadiens would go on to win the Stanley Cup, and Dryden would go on to a Hall of Fame career with Montreal.

His unforgettable performance against the Bruins, at the center of one of the NHL's biggest upsets, was a perfect start.

# 13

## DON'T EVER GIVE UP

Snapshots of the 1983 NCAA basketball finals:

- ✦ Jim Valvano's dash around the court
- ✦ Lorenzo Charles's "Dunk of Destiny"
- ✦ North Carolina State cutting down the net

Pictures worth preserving in any scrapbook of Wolfpack memories.

Final: North Carolina State 54, Houston 52. The "best team" had lost the NCAA championship.

The way the Wolfpack won the title was appropriate. They had been living on the edge for the last few weeks of the season. Close calls became their trademark. The team pulled out some nerve-racking games in the Atlantic Coast Conference tournament, and more in the NCAAs. They earned their nickname, the Cardiac Pack.

A "team of destiny" was an overworked expression in these

NCAAs. But if any team fit that description, it seemed to be the Wolfpack.

Frankly, no one had given North Carolina State a chance to do much of anything, not after finishing third in the ACC with an 8-6 record, 17-10 overall. The Wolfpack were off the radar screen when the regular season ended and the NCAA playoffs began.

The heavy favorite? Houston.

As the top-ranked team in the country for just about the whole season, the Cougars had earned that role.

The Cougars, nicknamed Phi Slamma Jamma, were a fearsome group of dunk-shot artists led by 7-foot Akeem (later changed to Hakeem) Olajuwon. The Cougars also featured Clyde "the Glide" Drexler, the nonpareil guard. And a transition game second to none.

The Cougars were rolling as they entered the tournament, with 22 straight victories.

North Carolina State was another story. There was only one way for the Wolfpack to qualify for the 52-team NCAA playoffs.

"We had to win the ACC tournament," guard Sidney Lowe said. "That was the only way we could get in."

So guess what! The Wolfpack beat Wake Forest by one point, Michael Jordan–led North Carolina in overtime, and Virginia with Ralph Sampson by three.

That opened the door to "the Big Dance" for North Carolina State. But the Wolfpack would shortly be waltzing right out—at least that was the consensus.

As their victories mounted in the tournament, however, people started thinking differently. They also started thinking about Jim Valvano, the Wolfpack's charismatic young coach, who somehow was finding a way to beat teams he wasn't supposed to challenge.

Valvano had always been a coach with a plan, not just for any particular game but for life itself.

But even though Valvano had mapped out his entire coaching career on index cards—five years here, five years there—nothing in life follows a set script. Certainly not in Valvano's life.

His story had all the highs and lows: top of the heap in the NCAAs, then a scandal involving NCAA violations that got him booted out of North Carolina State. He became even more popular as a broadcaster, but his life was cut short by cancer when he was at the top of his broadcasting game.

It could be called a tragic story. But knowing the positive-thinking Valvano, overall he would call it uplifting. And to many people it was.

"When I think of Jimmy, I think of him smiling," said Rick Barnes, who coached at Clemson when Valvano was at North Carolina State. "I think of him happy, holding court. You couldn't be around him without laughing."

Valvano always had good tales to tell, even if they were sometimes a little tall. One of his favorites:

"I asked a ref if he could give me a technical foul for thinking bad things about him. He said, of course not. I said, well, I think you stink. And he gave me the technical. You can't trust them."

He could be philosopher as well as funnyman.

"My father gave me the greatest gift anyone could give another person," Valvano once said. "He believed in me."

Born in New York City, Valvano was a very good college player at Rutgers. He wasn't going to be a pro, though.

So Valvano figured in very calculated steps how he could reach the top of the coaching profession.

First, a high school head coaching job, then a small college. He would go on to coach as an assistant at the university level, then he would be a head coach at a small university before finally landing his dream job of head coach at a major program.

He figured it would take him 20 years to reach the big time.

Somehow, Valvano reached his goal in 13 years, with stops at Johns Hopkins, Bucknell, and Iona before taking over the North Carolina State program in the 1980s. Valvano was brought to Raleigh to compete with North Carolina, the dominant team in the ACC, and win a national title.

Tommy Amaker, an assistant at Duke, recalled Valvano vividly as "a colorful, flamboyant coach. I remember him in Cameron [Duke's home court], taking his jacket off and flinging it down."

More to the point, Amaker also recalled that Valvano "always had good guards."

In the 1982–1983 season, the Wolfpack had excellent frontcourt players, led by Thurl Bailey. But their leadership came from the backcourt with Lowe and Dereck Whittenburg.

Still, the Wolfpack were getting no respect, even after winning the ACC tournament. In the NCAAs they were made a No. 6 seed and sent out to Corvallis, Oregon, to play in the West Regional.

"We were 20-10," Lowe said, "but the thing about it is that we played better than our record showed."

Whittenburg missed part of the season with a broken foot. "When he was there, we were pretty good," Lowe said.

It didn't appear the Wolfpack would last past the first round, though.

With just 28 seconds remaining in overtime, the Wolfpack trailed Pepperdine 59-55, and the Waves had one of their best free throw shooters, Dane Suttle, at the foul line.

Lowe, who had fouled out in regulation, was a sad figure on the bench.

"I was thinking, 'This can't be my last collegiate game. It's not supposed to end this way.'"

But Suttle missed the front end of a 1-and-1, and then Bailey scored a basket for North Carolina State.

Suttle had another chance to seal the game for Pepperdine, but he missed another 1-and-1 opportunity. He then fouled Whittenburg, giving North Carolina State a 1-and-1 of its own.

Whittenburg missed the first shot, but Cozell McQueen rebounded and scored to tie the game at 59.

In the second overtime, Whittenburg did better with his free throws, hitting 8 of 10 as North Carolina State pulled out a thrilling 69-67 victory.

"We had them beat, hanging-on-the-rope dead," Pepperdine coach Jim Harrick said. "They kept fouling us, and we kept missing."

Moving on, NC State played another thriller against Nevada-Las Vegas.

Ho hum, another day, another heart-stopper: The Wolfpack fell behind UNLV by 12 points in the second half but rallied to win 71-70. In both games, the Wolfpack won in the final seconds after their opponents failed at the foul line.

After beating Utah in an uncharacteristic blowout, North Carolina State reverted to form with a close win over ACC colleague Virginia in the West Regional final. Once again, the Wolfpack's opponent failed to take advantage of free throws. And once again, State won in the final seconds.

The tingling 63-62 victory over the Sampson Gang stunningly propelled the Wolfpack into the Final Four at Albuquerque, New Mexico.

Valvano joked that his team was playing in "the junior varsity game" against Georgia, another overachieving squad.

Meanwhile, No. 1 Houston faced No. 2 Louisville in the

# VIRGINIA'S HAWAIIAN HORROR SHOW

If it had been a book, it would have been pure fiction. A small NAIA school from Hawaii with no national reputation and not much of a history knocks off the nation's top-ranked NCAA Division I basketball team and its three-time player of the year.

Actually, it really did happen—to the Virginia Cavaliers and Ralph Sampson in 1982.

"What we did was amazing," said Chaminade coach Merv Lopes, recalling his team's historic 77-72 victory over Virginia a couple of days before Christmas that year.

The Cavaliers were making a stop in Hawaii to break up the trip home after a Christmas tournament in Japan. The last thing they expected was a tough time from Chaminade, a tiny school way out in the Pacific and far off the basketball radar screen.

"They had about as many students as Virginia had in the brass section of its band," one sports writer wisecracked about Chaminade, which had about 800 students.

A small student population and not much of a recruiting budget, either. Lopes said his budget for one season came to a grand total of $35. For road games on the island, the Silverswords traveled in an old Navy surplus van.

It had been only seven years earlier that Chaminade started playing intercollegiate basketball. The school didn't even have a campus all to itself; it had to share with bigger St. Louis High School.

Somehow, Lopes managed to turn out a winning program. In the 1982–1983 season, the Silverswords won 10 of their first 11 games, including a victory over Division I opponent Hawaii that Lopes had called "monumental."

However, Hawaii was no Virginia.

The Cavaliers were 8-0 after victories over national powerhouses Georgetown and Houston. The opening of the rugged Atlantic Coast Conference schedule wasn't far away. It appeared to basketball fans that Chaminade would be just a tune-up for the serious part of the Cavaliers' schedule.

They had every right to think that way.

With Sampson, the 7-foot-4 Lord High Executioner of the Cavaliers, Virginia had a player that dominated many a game.

After outplaying Georgetown's 7-foot star Patrick Ewing, Sampson didn't figure to have any trouble with Chaminade center Tony Randolph, nearly a foot shorter at 6-foot-6.

Sampson wasn't the only special player on a Cavaliers team generally regarded as the best all-around college squad in the country. The Cavaliers' stellar backcourt featured Rick Carlisle and Othell Wilson, two sharp-shooting, extremely quick guards.

The Silverswords, named for a rare plant found in Hawaiian volcanoes, got a rousing pregame pep talk from the colorful Lopes—described by one writer as "part Casey Stengel and part Phil Jackson."

Finally, Lopes had to deal with the reality of the situation.

"We're not going to win," he said. "Just go out and have some fun."

Reverse psychology? Maybe so. It seemed to work particularly well in Randolph's case. On their first possession, the Silverswords missed a shot, but Randolph followed with a dunk.

"I knew then that I was going to have a good game," he said. "The rim was huge that night. . . . I would fall down and the balls would still swish."

Randolph was giving up 10 inches and 80 pounds to Sampson, a player he faced in high school in Virginia. It didn't seem to matter.

"I knew what he was going to do," Randolph said. "It gave me confidence."

Randolph knew he couldn't handle Sampson inside, so he took him outside. And Randolph couldn't miss from there.

"He was letting me have that 19-foot jumper," Randolph said.

The Silverswords also showed they could dunk with flair, just like Virginia. On one play, they ran an alley-oop, with shooting guard Tim Dunham slamming the ball through the basket as Sampson gawked.

Virginia took a 7-point lead early in the second half, but Chaminade stayed close. With the help of Randolph and Dunham, the Silverswords went in front 64-62 late in the game.

With a minute and a half to play, it was 70-68 Chaminade. The

Cavaliers started fouling. The Silverswords continued hitting their free throws, clinching their stunning 5-point win.

Randolph finished with 19 points and added 5 rebounds. Sampson had 17 rebounds but was held to only 12 points on nine shots by a fierce Chaminade defense that forced 25 Virginia turnovers.

Some Hawaiian holiday.

The Cavaliers would go on to win a share of the ACC regular-season title before coming within one game of the Final Four and finishing with a 29-5 record.

Chaminade went on to the NAIA Final Four, where the Silverswords lost to the College of Charleston. But they could still look back on a season of great highlights, especially the monumental win over Virginia.

"Maybe we were lucky that it all came together that night," Randolph said in later years, "but I think it was meant to be."

generally perceived main event, a highly anticipated dunka-thon.

North Carolina State, which hadn't been ranked any higher than No. 15 in the polls during the season, beat Georgia 67-60.

That earned the Wolfpack the privilege of getting hammered in the finals by Houston, which thrashed Louisville 94-81. The Cougars couldn't have looked more dominant.

Lowe and Whittenburg watched on television as the Cougars set the tempo of the game from start to finish with their dash-and-dunk style. Phi Slamma Jammas, indeed.

"There were something like 22 dunks in that game [actually, Houston had 14]," Lowe said. "At one point, I looked over at Dereck and said, 'Oh, my God!'"

Valvano was watching on TV, too. He wasn't as awed as Lowe. Later, he told his players how they could beat the Cougars.

"We will have to control the tempo, keep the score in the 50s and 60s," Valvano said. "We want to be in a position to win it at the end."

Louisville had attempted to match Houston's speed with a pressing man-to-man defense. The Cardinals were unable to keep up with the Cougars, and by game's end were exhausted.

In the championship game, Valvano decided to go another way, using a collapsing zone defense that jammed the basket area and didn't allow the Cougars much room for their inside game.

"Most important, we didn't want them to get a dunk," said North Carolina State guard Terry Gannon. "Not one."

The North Carolina State players knew they had to play a perfect game to accomplish this. They received added motivation from an incident at practice the day before the game.

"The Houston guys showed up wearing Walkmen, sun glasses, sandals and shorts," Lowe said. "They acted as though they had the title won. Later, all of us got together. We were mad. We were fired up."

Before the game, Valvano had messages for each of his starters. To Lowe, he said:

"This is your last game ever. You're the finest point guard I've ever coached and tonight you are going to play flawlessly. You are going to go out there and handle the dish and play the game of your life and lead us to a national championship."

Not that the Wolfpack needed any motivational speeches from their coach.

"We never had an underdog attitude," said Lorenzo Charles, one of two sophomores in the Wolfpack's starting lineup.

That showed in the first half when North Carolina State set the tempo, as Valvano had suggested. The Wolfpack played at a disciplined pace—there was no shot clock in college basketball in 1983—and took only high-percentage shots. Most of them were falling, and at the half the Wolfpack had a stunning 33-25 lead.

"At halftime, I told the kids they were 20 minutes away," Valvano said. "I told them that we had a chance to do something that none of us would ever forget."

But suddenly in the second half, Houston's sleeping giant woke up. The Cougars, led by Olajuwon, went on a 17-2 tear to soar into the lead at 42-35 with about 10 minutes remaining. It was a typical lightning run by the Cougars, and visions of the Louisville rout began surfacing at the University of New Mexico's arena.

Just as suddenly, the Cougars inexplicably slowed down the game, going into their "locomotion offense."

Valvano was both mystified and pleased when Houston coach Guy Lewis decided to switch to a deliberate spread offense. It played directly into the Wolfpack's hands.

"I was a little surprised," Valvano said later. "They were on a roll. I don't know what was going through Coach Lewis's head."

Just this: "I wanted to pull State out and get some layups."

The move backfired.

"I remember looking up at the scoreboard and seeing us chip away at the lead," Charles said. "We knew all we needed to do was get into the last minute with a tie, and we would have the opportunity to pull the game out."

The Wolfpack defense forced a series of turnovers. Meanwhile, Whittenburg, Lowe, and Gannon provided some deadly outside shooting as NC State closed in on the Cougars. Whittenburg's 20-footer with 1:59 left tied the game at 52.

The Cougars could do nothing right, particularly at the foul line, where they missed a bunch of crucial shots in the final minutes. For all their talent, the Cougars were a notoriously poor foul shooting team. So Valvano wisely ordered his players to foul the Cougars.

The late-game strategy worked beautifully when Alvin Franklin missed a free throw that put the ball in the hands of the Wolfpack with 44 seconds left. Timeout, North Carolina State. Valvano told his players to hold the ball for a final, hopefully high-percentage, shot. But even the best-laid plans . . .

With precious seconds ticking away, Bailey was trapped in the corner and tossed a shaky pass out to Whittenburg at mid-court.

No time for a high-percentage shot now. With three seconds left, Whittenburg frantically whirled and let fly toward the basket from 35 feet.

"It wasn't the shot I wanted," Whittenburg said, "but I didn't want to go into overtime knowing I had the ball, but couldn't get the shot off."

It was off the mark. Way off.

But Charles was standing wide open under the basket. For some reason, Olajuwon hadn't boxed out his man.

"When I jumped, I thought the ball was short," remembered Charles. "But Akeem didn't see me. He just stood there. He didn't even go up."

Charles did. He slammed the ball through at the buzzer, climaxing yet another frantic finish for the Cardiac Pack. This one for a national championship.

Then Valvano made his fast break off the bench, arms opened wide, looking for someone to hug. Anyone to hug. After dozens of hugs, Valvano helped his team cut down the net.

Valvano was pretty much at a loss for words at the news conference.

*North Carolina State coach Jim Valvano celebrates the Wolfpack's
54-52 victory over Houston in the 1983 NCAA final.*

"I've got no funny lines," he said. "I'm almost speechless."

Maybe that was the best measure of how shocking this victory was: Motormouth Valvano left speechless.

Valvano's story didn't end in Albuquerque. In some ways, it
was the beginning of another journey.

Several years after winning the national title, Valvano was

investigated for NCAA violations for a multitude of wrong-doing involving his players. Some of Valvano's teams were also investigated for point-shaving. He eventually stepped down from his dual roles of athletic director and coach before becoming a media star as a basketball analyst.

Valvano was diagnosed with cancer in 1992. He went public with this very private disease, rallying new fans to his side. In 1993, he delivered a memorable speech at the ESPY Awards show when he was presented with the Arthur Ashe Award for Courage.

"Don't give up," he told the audience shortly before his death on April 28, 1993, "don't ever give up."

Valvano had wanted to leave a legacy, and he did. A foundation was set up in his name to raise money to fight cancer.

Another legacy: Valvano's philosophy of life, liberty, and the pursuit of basketball.

"The '83 team taught us about dreaming, and the importance of dreaming, that nothing can happen if not first the dream," he said years after leaving North Carolina State.

It's one of the reasons many midlevel teams go to the NCAA playoffs each year with the conviction that they, too, can be another North Carolina State.

# 14

## THE NEAR-PERFECT UPSET

It was 2005, and Rollie Massimino still couldn't bring himself to watch a complete videotape of the 1985 NCAA basketball finals. The reason?

"I still think we might lose," the former Villanova coach said in an interview on the 20th anniversary of the Wildcats' improbable 66-64 victory over Georgetown.

Massimino couldn't be blamed for thinking that way, even 20 years after the fact. Very few believed the Wildcats could beat this deeply talented Georgetown team headed by Patrick Ewing, the country's best center and a future first overall pick in the NBA draft.

The glowering 7-foot Ewing was inviting comparisons to the great Bill Russell when he played for the University of San Francisco some 30 years before. And Georgetown had four other players ticketed by NBA scouts as potential first-round draft choices: Michael Jackson, Reggie Williams, Billy Martin, and David Wingate.

Villanova had only one, according to the scouts: center Ed Pinckney.

"The thing that makes it very memorable is the fact absolutely nobody picked us to win it, even our parents," Pinckney recalled. "My parents before the game were sort of preparing me to take a loss. They're saying, 'You don't have to worry about this game. If you don't win, you got this far. . . .'"

Massimino was thinking otherwise. Before tip-off, he told his team: "We're gonna win."

If Massimino had any kind of talent as a coach, it was making his "kids," as he called them, believe in themselves. Once an assistant coach at Penn, Massimino nurtured a family atmosphere on his Villanova teams. His players appreciated both his approach to basketball and to life. Massimino had been on his way to Italy to coach basketball when he was interviewed for the Villanova job.

"I took the job without even seeing Villanova," he said. "It was my dream job."

For many years at Villanova, Massimino was a beloved figure—at least for Wildcats fans and players. Officials might have thought otherwise when they saw Massimino's disheveled figure stomping his feet and racing up and down the sideline to holler at them.

Nor would he change his style when later coaching Cleveland State, where he had a less successful run than at Villanova. As it was, nothing he ever did before or afterward could match the artistic success of the 1985 championship season with the Wildcats. And no team was ever closer to his heart.

The Hoyas in the 1984–1985 season were considered far and wide the best team in the country. The Wildcats were only the fourth-best team in the Big East and had already lost twice in two meetings with Georgetown that season.

The Hoyas were making their third appearance in four years

in the national finals and were gunning for their second straight national championship.

The Wildcats weren't even sure they would make it into the tournament.

In previous years, the Wildcats' 19-10 record might not have been good enough for the NCAA playoffs. More likely they would have gone to the less-prestigious NIT. But the NCAA tournament had just been expanded to 64 teams, and the Wildcats were content with any seeding they could get. As it was, they were placed a lowly No. 8.

Villanova had gone 6-5 in its last 11 games of the season, hardly a noteworthy accomplishment. The Wildcats' mediocre record included an 85-62 pounding by Pitt in the last game of the season.

The loss actually appeared to be a turning point for Villanova. The Wildcats had played so poorly against Pitt that Massimino was infuriated. Forward Dwayne McClain remembered that at halftime Massimino "told us we had three minutes to prove ourselves."

They didn't do so, as far as Massimino was concerned. And at the 17-minute mark, the frustrated coach pulled his entire starting lineup off the floor.

"Coach was trying to teach us a lesson, that we can't just turn it on whenever we want to," McClain said.

Not unless you were Georgetown, which seemed to do just that during an overpowering season.

The 1984–1985 campaign had been a battle between the Hoyas and St. John's for the Big East lead, not to mention the No. 1 ranking in the country. St. John's had beaten Georgetown in their first meeting, but late in the season the Hoyas established their supremacy with a 16-point rout of the Redmen.

Syracuse, another nationally ranked Big East colleague, was the only other team to beat Georgetown. But the Hoyas

# DUKE DOES IN RUNNIN' REBELS

Before playing UNLV in the 1991 NCAA championship semifinals, the Duke basketball team watched a horror video.

It wasn't a movie—it was the tape of the 1990 NCAA championship game in which UNLV had thrashed the Blue Devils by 30 points in the biggest blowout in finals history.

The reason Duke Coach Mike Krzyzewski pulled out the year-old tape and made his team watch the first six minutes?

He wanted to show the difference between a team that played with energy and emotion (UNLV) and one that played without any spark at all (Duke).

"This was one of the few games where we actually came back a year later and talked about a team to our guys," said assistant coach Pete Gaudet. "Usually, it's water over the dam."

With NBA-style players Greg Anthony, Larry Johnson, Stacey Augmon, and Anderson Hunt, the top-ranked Rebels were explosive and quick. A team of veterans, they usually toyed with opponents while running up a 45-game winning streak over two seasons.

"They want to make you look like third-graders running around at recess," said Utah coach Rick Majerus.

The Blue Devils, meanwhile, had lost three senior starters to graduation. They had a youthful lineup, with many prominent roles assigned to underclassmen, including freshman forward Grant Hill. Hill had been in high school the year the Rebels ran the Blue Devils out of the arena. Now he was in the starting lineup, facing many of the same players from UNLV's 1990 national-title team.

Another title for UNLV was just considered a matter of time.

"Everybody had already issued championship rings for that [1990–1991] team," Duke broadcaster Bob Harris said.

For Duke point guard Bobby Hurley, the game was especially personal. Now a senior, he had been living with vivid memories of his poor performance against UNLV in 1990. He said he had nightmares about sharks—which sounded somewhat Freudian. "Shark," of course, was the nickname of Runnin' Rebels coach Jerry Tarkanian.

"That had to be because of UNLV," Hurley said. "I'd dream I was in a swimming pool with sharks all around me. Sometimes I'd get away by jumping out, but other times I'd stay in. I wasn't scared."

Hurley was constantly being reminded by friends of the embarrassing loss in 1990.

"I couldn't even look them in the eye when I talked about the game, because it was so humiliating," Hurley said.

Hurley did not want to fail again, and he especially did not want to repeat the worst performance of his college career (two points, three assists, and five turnovers in the 103-73 rout).

It was also personal for Krzyzewski, who had rarely been subjected to such an embarrassing loss.

"Our goal this week is to get a little bit better, so we can come within 30 on Saturday," the Duke coach told reporters with a grin.

Actually, Krzyzewski said one thing to the media and something else to his team. He fully believed his Blue Devils could beat this slick college basketball juggernaut from Las Vegas. They would need to play a perfect game to do it, that's all.

And so they would.

Hill's dunk shot at the start was a confidence builder for the Blue Devils. So was his play against Augmon, one of UNLV's senior leaders and the three-time national defensive player of the year. Hill also helped guard other players in Duke's defensive schemes.

Christian Laettner, just beginning to solidify his reputation as a clutch shooter, couldn't miss from the field. Nor could reserve Brian Davis.

Also significant was the play of Hurley. Standing up to "the sharks" and "the Shark," he redeemed himself with 12 points, seven assists, and only three turnovers in 40 minutes of play.

With 12 seconds to play, Laettner clinched it for the Blue Devils with two free throws that gave him 28 points for the game.

Final: Duke 79, UNLV 77.

Two nights later, the Blue Devils beat Kansas for the national championship.

Now Hurley could face his friends again without embarrassment, and the Blue Devils could finally look at themselves in the mirror. And see champions looking back.

avenged that loss with a 27-point thrashing of the Orangemen in the last game of the regular season and took over the No. 1 spot.

The Hoyas cemented their position by winning the Big East tournament title, knocking off St. John's by 12 points in the championship game to improve to 30-2.

That meant bad news for opponents in the upcoming NCAAs.

"I think this team is as good as last year's," Georgetown coach John Thompson said in an uncharacteristic boast.

St. John's assistant coach Brian Mahoney thought so, too. Maybe better.

"The only team that can beat Georgetown is maybe Georgetown," he said.

On the way to the Final Four, there were a couple of surprises: Villanova upset Michigan, the No. 2 ranked team in the country, and Georgia Tech nearly upset Georgetown.

"Finding a way to win; that's what champions are all about," Thompson said after the Hoyas squeezed by Georgia Tech 60-54.

Villanova found a way, too, winning 59-55 over Michigan with the help of a system of baffling zone defenses.

"I guess playing in that league, they didn't face too many good zones," Villanova's Harold Pressley said of the Big Ten, which generally favored man-to-man defenses. "We kept changing our zones and they didn't understand what we were doing."

Then came a message from another Villanova player that would be prophetic:

"There's nothing gonna intimidate us," said guard Gary McLain.

Massimino made sure his team continued to play tight defense but at the same time stayed loose mentally. At the halftime of the regional final against North Carolina, the Wildcats trailed the Tar Heels when Massimino made one of his more memorable locker room speeches. This one is long remembered in Villanova lore as "the Spaghetti Speech."

Massimino ripped off his jacket and threw it on the floor. Then he started screaming and yelling about wanting a big bowl of pasta more than he wanted a national championship.

He talked about the delicious clam sauce he was going to put on the pasta, and then the cheese.

"We're looking at him like he's nuts," said Rob Wilson, then a team manager. "Nobody knew how to take it."

The message did ultimately get through, though.

"I finally realized that he was saying, 'You guys are taking this way too serious. You're uptight. You just need to relax.'"

The "relaxed" Wildcats took care of the Tar Heels and advanced to the Final Four. It was a Big East show, with Georgetown, Villanova, and St. John's among the group. Memphis State completed the field.

No question which team was top dog.

"Not since the UCLA run [10 championships in 12 years from 1964–1975] has there been such an odds-on favorite," coaching legend Al McGuire wrote about Georgetown in the *Los Angeles Times*.

The Hoyas followed expectations by trouncing St. John's 77-59 to gain the NCAA finals for the third time in four years.

"It's really a great team," St. John's coach Lou Carnesecca remarked to one of his assistants in the final minutes of the Hoyas' victory.

Later, Carnesecca told reporters: "They're not just physical. They're just good. They have such flexibility offensively."

The red-hot Hoyas looked invincible as they charged into the championship game with a 17-game winning streak.

Villanova, meanwhile, continued to be the surprise of the

tournament. The Wildcats survived against Memphis State 52-45 in the other national semifinal game.

"Maybe," Massimino said, "it's just destiny."

But unless "destiny" could play defense, Villanova wasn't given even the slightest chance of dethroning a Georgetown team that Carnesecca had called one of the greatest ever.

"It Would Take an N.C. State-Type Miracle to Unseat Hoyas Tonight," headlined the *Los Angeles Times*.

The newspaper made reference to North Carolina State's shocking victory over Houston in 1983, then considered the greatest upset in NCAA finals history.

It was hard for the Wildcats not to be intimidated, even though they had played Georgetown tough during the regular season and were familiar with the Hoyas' style.

"I can't tell you how mentally prepared you had to be to play against that team," Pinckney said.

Pinckney was given the daunting task of trying to contain Ewing, who was three inches taller. The Villanova center would not be doing the assignment under the best of circumstances, either.

As Massimino remembered, "He was sick that Sunday and Monday of the final game."

Pinckney looked better once the game began. And simply great near the end.

In the first half, the Wildcats connected on 13 of 18 shots and led 29-28. They continued to sharp-shoot over the Hoyas, and with Villanova trailing late in the game, Pinckney hit a shot over Ewing to put the Wildcats back in front. He later made two free throws. And then he drove on the great Georgetown center to make a jump shot for a 53-48 Villanova lead.

Back came the Hoyas to go ahead 54-53.

With about three minutes left, Georgetown decided to

spread the court. But the strategy backfired when the Hoyas turned over the ball.

The Wildcats then went into their own slowdown offense.

"We held the ball for 35 seconds," Massimino said. "We weren't afraid to lose. We were playing to win."

Harold Jensen, a reserve guard, then scored on a jump shot to give the Wildcats a lead they never lost. Jensen's five-for-five shooting was typical of the accuracy displayed by the Villanova players.

The Wildcats put on an amazing shooting display, particularly after intermission. They missed one shot—one shot!—in the entire second half, making 9 of 10 from the field. From the foul line, Villanova connected on 22 of 27 free throws overall.

The field goal accuracy of 78.6 percent broke the NCAA championship game record of 67.4 set by Ohio State against California in 1960. It was also a record for the tournament.

That incredible shooting display, coupled with a skintight defense, carried the unheralded Wildcats to a two-point victory over the stunned Hoyas. Before a stunned nation.

When it was over, Massimino, even more disheveled than normal, had one of the most unpredictable championships in sports history.

"Ninety percent—that's unbelievable," said Georgetown's Jackson of the Wildcats' second-half shooting percentage. "They hit their shots, hit their free throws and kept coming at us. We didn't give them anything. They earned it."

The Wildcats knew they had to be very nearly perfect to beat Georgetown, and they were.

"Every player wants to sort of have their masterpiece," said Pinckney, who earned the tournament's outstanding player award. "That team has that. We put our signature on a great game and went out in a great way."

# 15

## ORVILLE'S OPEN

Orville Moody. Not exactly a name to conjure fear among the competition.

Indeed, Bill Murray's character in *Caddyshack* easily could have been named Orville Moody. So might the president of the local Kiwanis Club.

When the 1969 U.S. Open was played at the steamy Cypress Creek Course of the Champions Golf Club in Houston, Moody was even a longer shot than the man who scored a surprising win the year before, Lee Trevino. And after Moody outlasted a group of outsiders to capture America's most prestigious golfing title—it was not a good Open for such favorites as Jack Nicklaus, Arnold Palmer, and Trevino—headlines screamed, "Orville Who?"

Well, Orville Who wouldn't be much of a factor in other major events on the PGA Tour during a career that spanned four decades. Although he had a solid stint on the Seniors

Tour, even winning another major there, the 1969 upset always has carried the tag "fluke."

Moody liked to joke that there were a half-dozen officers in the Army who could beat him on a given day. But the former staff sergeant was the only military man to emerge from service, in 1967, and almost immediately qualify for the PGA Tour.

That, in itself, was quite an achievement for the 14-year Army vet, considering Moody was 34 at the time and playing against younger golfers who were trained not for fighting wars but for breaking par.

Moody also wasn't fine-tuned in the pressure situations the tour regulars faced each week. He'd won such tournaments as the Korean Open, hardly a top-level event in the 1960s, as well as dozens of military events. But his first full season on the PGA Tour had been something of a struggle.

Oh, and one more thing: He couldn't putt.

"A guy that nobody ever thinks of who could do a lot of things with the golf ball was Orville Moody," said Bob Rosburg, a longtime golf TV commentator and a former PGA Championship winner (1959). "If he'd been able to putt, there's no telling how many tournaments he would have won."

Fred Couples, a master putter when he starred on the tour in the 1990s, recalled going to watch the pros in the 1970s and how Moody "pretty much just slapped the ball around on the greens."

Added Moody himself: "Jack Nicklaus and Lee, those are great putters. You wouldn't put my name in there with them."

For one weekend in June 1969, you could.

Moody had to go through sectional qualifying just to get into the Open, which is, well, open to any high-quality golfer, professional or amateur. This is the one U.S. tournament in which the magicians on tour might compete with the assistant golf pro from the municipal course or against the high school hotshot.

Moody passed that test thanks to sinking a bunker shot for a birdie, but after shooting the highest qualifying score to make the Open, he wasn't mentioned in any of the tournament previews as a contender. Indeed, his only previous Open appearance was in 1962, the year Nicklaus won his first of 18 pro majors. Moody? He didn't even make the cut.

He was more likely to miss the cut again than win in Houston.

"I didn't go into the tournament thinking about what it would be like to win the U.S. Open," he said. "I went there to play some good golf in a major tournament and see if I could build on that."

Someone else was expecting Moody to do plenty at Champions. Trevino, who served in the Marines and had competed against Moody in military tournaments, surveyed the field, examined the course and conditions, then said: "If I don't win, I think Orville Moody will win."

Trevino, of course, became known for his quick wit and his willingness to bet on almost anything involving a golf ball. But even for Trevino, this was an outlandish prediction.

Moody shot 71 in the first round, the same score as such luminaries as Gary Player, Johnny Miller, Julius Boros, and Tony Jacklin, all of whom would own Open titles at some point in their illustrious careers.

But Moody's atrocious putting bothered playing partners Jacklin and Dale Douglass so much that they insisted he join them on the practice green after the round.

It must have helped. After a par-70 in the second round, Moody was tied with Miller, Jacklin, and the great Nicklaus, four strokes behind Deane Beman, well within range. And after a steady 68 in the third round, the names at the very top of the

# FLECK'S OPEN SURPRISE

Ben Hogan was his idol. That didn't stop Jack Fleck from toppling the great golfer at the 1955 U.S. Open.

While Hogan was a heroic figure for overcoming a nearly fatal automobile accident in 1949 to again win major titles, Fleck was such an obscure pro that, even though he claimed to have invented the practice of pacing off yardage to measure shot distances, "I was just too unknown to be given credit for it."

Hogan was at the top of his game—and the top of the golf world—when the 1955 Open came to the Olympic Club in San Francisco. From 1948 through 1953, he'd won the event four times. It was custom made for his sweet swing and intense nature.

While Hogan had befriended Fleck, even taking him on a tour of the factory that manufactured Hogan's clubs—something few other tour pros ever did—Hogan wasn't about to back off against him, or anyone. Ironically, though, Hogan helped Fleck's game that week by hand-delivering two wedges made for Fleck by his company.

After Fleck opened with a 76, he seemed hopelessly behind. But he fared better in the second round with a 69 to make the cut.

While shaving before the 36-hole final day, Fleck insisted he heard a voice proclaim: "Jack, you're going to win the Open." Instead of being shaken, he said he became inspired. At times, he even referred to the voice as "an angel."

Popping sugar cubes during the rounds, Fleck again seemed out of contention after a 75 on the first 18. But he got hot in the final round and found himself just one stroke behind the leader, Hogan, through 13 holes of Saturday's second 18.

"I proceeded to bogey the 14th," he recalled. "But I knew I was playing well and I wasn't real tired or anything, even with all the holes we played. I thought I could make two birdies to tie Ben, at least."

Coming down the stretch of any major, particularly the U.S. Open with its high rough, tight fairways, and speedy greens, is difficult enough. Chasing the great Hogan, well, that's a near-impossible assignment.

Not for the journeyman from Iowa.

"I birdied 15," he said, "and then someone told me that network television had signed off, saying Ben was the winner. I had to laugh at that one."

On 18, needing a birdie for a 67 that would force an 18-hole playoff, Fleck hit a 3-wood (a Ben Hogan model, no less) off the tee and then a 7-iron within seven feet of the pin. With a pure stroke, he knocked the putt straight into the hole.

The playoff was expected to be an afterthought, a rout. Hogan not only was the fiercest competitor in golf, but he also carried an aura that intimidated even the best opponents. You simply didn't stare down Ben Hogan.

Yet Fleck felt no such intimidation. Indeed, he said he was so relaxed that he never thought twice about losing.

He never came close to losing, either. Hogan played well enough, shooting a 72, but Fleck, sticking his approach shots close on nearly every hole, posted a 69 in his third 18-hole round in 24 hours.

The loss signaled the end of Hogan's dominant ways on tour. The Texan never won another major.

For Fleck, meanwhile, it would be the only major championship in his resume, underscoring one of the greatest upsets in golf history.

board were Miller, Barber, and Moody, who was three strokes behind.

Moody's third-round score, his best so far in the Open, was even more remarkable because his caddie, a 17-year-old high school senior named Michael Ashe, inadvertently had dropped his yardage marker in a toilet before the round. That would be tantamount to a football player losing his playbook during the week before the Super Bowl, and most caddies would have been fired on the spot.

Ashe figured he was done at the Open.

"I almost cried," Ashe said. "You know, I could have cost Mr. Moody the tournament.

"But Mr. Moody laughed when I told him about it. He said, 'Don't worry.' He wasn't going to let it bother him, and he wanted me to do the same, not be bothered."

Moody was staying close because his putting wasn't undermining the rest of his game. From tee to green, Moody was a precisionist, with a smooth stroke and a patient approach. But he usually had difficulty reading putts and judging their speed. In fact, later in his career, on the Seniors Tour, Moody would make a lasting impression—and contribution—by switching to an elongated 50-inch putter.

With that putter, he would win the 1989 Senior Players Championship and finish second in earnings with $647,985.

"I've had such a bad reputation on three and four-footers," Moody said. "There were times in the past when I'd hit 18 greens in regulation and walk away with 71. I'd give away three or four shots a round, and I'm convinced I could have won a lot more money if I'd been able to putt."

Yet, in the 1969 Open, the guy could putt.

Entering the final round, Moody was somewhat comforted that he wasn't chasing any of the big names of golf. He also would have a decent gallery because he was from nearby Oklahoma. But Barber was a Texan, which meant most of the fans on this sticky-hot June day would be in Barber's corner.

Then Barber let Moody off the hook by struggling from the outset. While "Sarge" was in charge of his game, Barber was butchering the course en route to a 78.

That left the likes of Beman (the future PGA Tour commissioner), Rosburg, and Al Geiberger as his main obstacles to an unimaginable championship.

"I don't think Mr. Moody ever thought about the pressure of that situation, of winning the national Open," Ashe said. "He just kept playing his game."

Indeed, Moody seemed made for this moment. Par-busting scores don't happen much in the Open, especially on a course like Champions in 100-degree heat. Even par is a good score, often a winning score in the Open.

In fact, Moody would make only six birdies and an eagle, but he stayed away from trouble with just nine bogeys. No double bogeys or triples, as other, more heralded players had made. No 7s or 8s.

"I knew I could hit the fairways, stay out of trouble, and make pars," Moody said. "That could be good enough."

He was correct. After 17 exhausting holes, if Moody could make a par-4 on the tough 18th, he would finish at 1-over-par 281 and outlast the impressive field to post his first win as a pro. In the U.S. Open, no less.

Moody sent his drive down the middle of the fairway, as he'd done time and again for four days. Standing with an 8-iron, he didn't take a lot of time surveying the landscape—or his chances. He knocked the ball about 15 feet from the hole.

Two putts and he would be the Open champion.

But, remember, this was a man who dubbed himself "a horrible putter" on more than one occasion.

"He remained confident," Ashe said. "He believed that a two-putt from that distance would not be a problem."

Moody's first putt came up about a foot short. A tap-in—normally.

But now he was beginning to think about what those last inches would mean if he stroked the ball into the hole. Moody looked at the putt from several angles before addressing the ball. He seemed to freeze over the putt for minutes, which must have felt like hours to him. Actually, it was perhaps a dozen seconds or so . . . and then he holed it.

"That was a long 14-incher," he said. "A million dollar 14-incher."

He was right on that account. Moody, whose asking price

was minuscule as an endorser before the Open, would be worth significantly more. His story was uplifting, his military background was inspiring. He's the last player to go through qualifying and win the Open.

His agent, Bucky Woy, estimated that Moody's price tag had gone from $5,000 to perhaps 20 times that.

Moody wouldn't win again on the regular tour but had far more success as a Seniors player. He will always be remembered as the long-shot champion at Champions.

# 16

## WALTRIP'S GREAT AMERICAN UPSET: TRIUMPH AND TRAGEDY AT DAYTONA

Michael Waltrip was on one hellacious ride.

Since 1986, when he began his career in stock car racing's top show, then called the Winston Cup, Waltrip hadn't won a points race. Even though he was the runner-up for rookie of the year in 1986 and performed decently in 1991, 1994, and 1996, the only time he took the checkered flag was for the 1996 Winston, an all-star race and glorified exhibition featuring some wild driving.

For more than a decade, Waltrip was saddled with either underfinanced teams or mediocre crews, often both. He hardly was a candidate to win the Great American Race.

Indeed, in 462 career starts entering the 2001 season, Waltrip's best finish had been a second way back in 1988. He certainly wasn't in the class of older brother Darrell, a Hall of Famer who won three series championships and 84 races.

What he did have was an engaging personality, a self-deprecating sense of humor, good looks, and a deep knowledge of what race cars are supposed to do. He simply couldn't get them to do those things well enough for a trip to Victory Lane.

"I always felt I was good enough to be here and to compete," he said. "I just hadn't won, and that's what this sport is all about, getting into the winner's circle."

Waltrip had befriended many of stock car racing's power brokers and stars, including Dale Earnhardt, perhaps the greatest driver in NASCAR history. Earnhardt, owner of seven Cup championships, was driving for Richard Childress Racing in 2000, but he'd also begun his own stable, Dale Earnhardt Inc. In part, Earnhardt started DEI to provide his son, Dale Jr., with a Cup ride. Junior already was a champion in the second-level Busch circuit, and he joined the Winston Cup parade full time in 2000.

But DEI had other cars to fill, and one job was held by Steve Park. The other spot was open.

"Dale asked me about driving for him, and, well, it wasn't a difficult decision," Waltrip admitted just before the 2001 Daytona 500. "In the early '90s, I was satisfied as a driver because I knew when I went to the racetrack I might win. In the last few years, it hasn't been that way. Now, I think coming to this team is my best chance to win in a long time.

"The sport has changed a lot and it's harder now, but this team has everything you need to win. Some people never get the chance to show what they can do. I'm in a position to be successful. I understand all the pressure and I understand this organization. You're looking at one happy dude."

Earnhardt was happy, too. Not just because he was helping a friend but because he was convinced Waltrip could bring home the No. 15 Napa Chevrolet at the head of the field.

"I hired Michael because I believe he's a talented driver who can help this team," Earnhardt said. "If I felt he couldn't win, he wouldn't be here."

The Daytona 500 is NASCAR's biggest race, and unlike golf and tennis, which save many of their showcases for midseason or later, the race kicks off the stock car season. The previous schedule ends in November, leaving teams more than two months to begin preparing for the 500.

That includes building teams—crew chiefs, car chiefs, engineers, pit workers, spotters—as well as cars. Waltrip was familiar with the process, but he had much to learn at DEI.

For instance, he needed to get a feel for the cars. How would they handle in traffic or up front in clean air? How much horsepower could the engines produce? How well could he mesh his driving style with the machine he was piloting?

Almost as critical would be how well Waltrip could work with Dale Jr. and Park in the 500. Because NASCAR requires restrictor plates on the carburetors at Daytona, the cars tend to race in packs. They draft with each other, tearing a hole in the air as they circle the two-and-a half-mile track. It's essential that a driver have help from another car or two or even a whole line of autos, or else he will be "hung out to dry" on his own.

Both Earnhardt Jr. and Waltrip knew they would have fast cars for the race. That was evident from the beginning of Speed Week, the week leading up to the Great American Race.

"Oh, we'll get around here quick," Junior said. "If Michael and I can hang together and get in a good draft and get to the front, we'll be plenty fast enough."

Waltrip began the race in the 19th spot among 43 cars. Dale Jr. was in the 6th slot, while Park started 25th. Earnhardt himself was 7th on the grid.

If Waltrip had finished 19th in the race, nobody would have been shocked. Except, perhaps, Waltrip.

"We've got a car that can compete," he said. "Just watch."

Watching from the broadcast booth was his older brother. NASCAR had just signed a lucrative television deal with Fox, NBC, and TNT. Fox had the first half of the schedule, including the Daytona 500. Making his debut as the main analyst for Fox was none other than Darrell Waltrip.

In his prerace comments, the colorful DW didn't play up his brother's chances. Frankly, the former NASCAR star wasn't sure how "Mikey" would fair. He certainly wasn't among the favorites, a role reserved for the elder Earnhardt, defending champion Dale Jarrett, and Jeff Gordon.

Fox applied the usual hyperbole to its broadcast, hoping to introduce a touch of Hollywood to the good ol' boys of NASCAR. In no way did it expect to present one of the greatest upsets in sports history.

And one of the most tragic endings.

By midway through the 200 laps, it had become clear the DEI cars were stout. Both Waltrip and Dale Jr. were up among the leaders, if not out front altogether, and they'd managed to avoid the trouble that always seems to come at Daytona.

Late in the day, a spectacular 19-car crash eliminated nearly half the field. That included Tony Stewart, whose fiery car went airborne. Stewart escaped with a sore shoulder and a concussion, which seemed miraculous to anyone who saw No. 20 hurtle down the track. The size of the melee was so big that NASCAR halted the race under a red flag in order to clear the track.

The lead group featured both Earnhardts, Waltrip, Rusty Wallace, Ken Schrader, and Sterling Marlin. With the exception of Junior, all were NASCAR veterans familiar with the quirks of the steeply banked, very fast Daytona track. Earnhardt was the most successful of drivers at the prestigious facility, although he'd won only one 500, in 1998. Marlin had captured two Daytona 500s, while Schrader was always a factor on the superspeedways.

Dale Jr. had shown he understood the dynamics of restrictor-plate racing during his years in the Busch series. The only seeming interlopers in the lead pack were Wallace, who despite being one of the all-time greats of the sport had never won at Daytona, and Waltrip.

But heading into the final 26 laps, Waltrip was a factor. And as the laps wound down, it became clear that one of the DEI entries, either Dale Jr. or Waltrip, was the car to beat.

Wallace, though, was on the move, showing enough speed and power to sneak into the lead. Marlin and Schrader also looked strong.

Earnhardt, who some opponents said could sense where the pockets of clean air were in restrictor-plate events, was sitting just behind his buddy and his son as what was left of the field reached the white flag. One lap to go. Decision time.

Earnhardt kept his black No. 3 Chevrolet, by far the most popular and recognizable machine in auto racing, behind Junior's No. 8, which trailed Waltrip's No. 15. "The Intimidator" was going to be "the Protector," blocking the other contenders just enough so they couldn't reach Dale Jr. or Waltrip.

The man who hired the underaccomplished Michael Waltrip was ensuring him his first true Winston Cup win.

Earnhardt never made a move to challenge the two cars he owned. As they left the backstretch, Earnhardt drifted toward the bottom of the track, where Marlin was running. They touched, and Earnhardt's car headed directly toward the outside wall in Turn 4.

Schrader was on the outside and could not avoid Earnhardt as the No. 3 careered into the wall nose-first. Schrader, a close friend of Earnhardt's, plowed into his side.

Fox's cameras did not capture any of this live because,

rightly so, they were concentrated on what was happening up front: Waltrip leading Dale Jr. to the finish line. In the broadcast booth, Darrell Waltrip was rooting his little brother on, exhorting Mikey to keep doing exactly what he had done for the first 199 laps.

The viewer could almost sense Darrell squirming in the booth, applying his own body language as if he were in the driver's seat.

And when Waltrip took the checkered flag for his first career win—in the Daytona 500, no less!—Darrell's voice cracked with emotion.

"You got it, you got it!" DW exclaimed. "All right. It's a television dream come true. Oh, man!"

But DW also recognized immediately the potential severity of the crash on the final turn. While praising his brother for his perseverance, Darrell said he was praying for his former rival's safety.

Waltrip immediately took what could have been the most satisfying victory lap NASCAR had seen since, well, since Dale Earnhardt finally won the 500 three years earlier. He was aware that his new boss had been running interference for him and that there had been a crash seconds before he crossed the finish line. But car racers, while not immune to the inherent dangers of their profession, prefer to downplay the danger.

As Waltrip made his way to Victory Lane, track workers feverishly were trying to help Earnhardt, whose car had slid into the infield. Schrader already had climbed from his mangled machine and hustled over to Earnhardt's car to check on him.

"Out of compassion for his friend, he went to the car and I think maybe he saw more than what he bargained for," Schrader's wife, Ann, told the Associated Press. "But at the same time, he takes comfort in that one of the last people Dale might have seen and heard was Kenny, a friend who was there for him."

Getty Images

*Michael Waltrip following his Daytona 500 win in 2001.*

Waltrip would be robbed of having his friend—and career saver—there for him in the winner's circle. While Waltrip was doing interviews, Earnhardt was cut out of his auto and placed in an ambulance.

"I owe this all to Dale Jr. And his daddy, too," Waltrip said. "I saw him back there fighting them off. I know they're all very proud of their driver."

Waltrip held up his arm, his fingers forming a V for victory. He fully expected both Earnhardts to join him any moment for the celebration.

But Dale Jr. was headed to the hospital to be with his father. Instead, it was Schrader who came to Waltrip's side.

"I didn't know what the final deal was, so I just told him it was big and Dale was in trouble," Schrader said. "It was Mikey's biggest moment, and you're adding news that he doesn't want. But I knew he'd want to know."

While Waltrip went on with the obligatory interviews, there was no more celebrating, only consternation and concern. He might have dreamed of winning the big race more times than he had circled the track, but at this time, under these circumstances, his huge upset hardly felt the way it should have.

"My heart is hurting right now," he said. "I would rather be any place right this moment than here. It's so painful."

Waltrip fully understood how much his friend Earnhardt helped him to this win, making it even more painful.

"He was just doing his job," he said. "Close racing sometimes makes contact happen and sometimes contact happens with the wall. I don't think anyone could have done anything any different in that situation to help Dale."

Moments later, when NASCAR president Mike Helton told the world of Earnhardt's death, he said the sports world "lost one of its greatest competitors and great friends." In the succeeding days, the outpouring of respect and love for the Intimidator overshadowed everything else on the sports calendar.

By his own estimation, Michael Waltrip cried "thousands of tears" in the succeeding days. Never did he mention how unfair it all was, how he never could fully thank Earnhardt. Or about how his great triumph was virtually ignored.

Because racers always move on, the circuit headed to Rockingham, North Carolina, the next weekend. After Earnhardt's funeral, Waltrip and Dale Jr., Schrader and Marlin—everyone—got back to racing.

"My personal thinking is that when this weekend is over, and we've raced, then next week we can talk about winning the Daytona 500," Waltrip said. "It's just my personal preference to let this week be the week that we just talk about Dale and what he meant to all of us."

Eventually, Waltrip certainly would get the proper recognition for his achievement. Indeed, he would win another Daytona 500 in 2003, although this one was cut short by rain. And anytime he contended in subsequent races, particularly at restrictor-plate tracks, it was no surprise.

But on February 18, 2001, Waltrip's win was a shocker. Unfortunately, that Daytona 500 will never be remembered for his steering the No. 15 to the checkered flag.

# 17

## CHANG TAKES PARIS BY STORM

The searing pain began in his legs. It worked its way through his body. On the verge of one of the great comebacks and upsets in tennis history, 17-year-old Michael Chang looked like an old man, bent over and hobbling.

Even worse, that's how he felt.

And the man on the other side of the net in the fourth round at the 1989 French Open, top-ranked Ivan Lendl, wasn't about to let anyone slide—particularly this young American who ran down every ball and never stopped battling.

Lendl sometimes was deemed "a cold assassin" on the tennis court, but if his game couldn't handle Chang on this day, he'd let fatigue and dehydration do the job.

"When I started to cramp, I knew that the longer the points went, the harder it would be for me to win," Chang said. "If I put any pressure on any muscle, I would cramp immediately. I did everything I could to win as many points as possible. When I had a chance, I went for it."

What Chang went for—and got—was a dramatic victory that Hollywood couldn't scheme up. And it propelled him to even further sensational achievements.

Chang came to Paris with no illusions of grandeur at Roland Garros. Although the youngest player in the Open field—and among the shortest at 5-foot-8—Chang had little trouble in his first three matches, but he knew Lendl presented the most formidable obstacle of his two-plus-year pro career. While Chang had beaten Lendl in an exhibition match in Atlanta weeks earlier, he drew little confidence from that meeting.

"Lendl's not going to mess around now," he said. "This is the real thing. You can see it in his face. He has that look. He doesn't give you anything."

The dour Lendl even managed a smile when reminded of the previous loss to Chang.

"The last time I had been playing only four days on clay," he said. "This time I've been playing for six weeks on clay. That's the difference and the result will be different, too."

Lendl was among the favorites in the event, having already won three championships on Paris's red clay. Chang, while seeded 15th, was a long shot known best for his energy and willingness to slug it out from the baseline.

But that strategy rarely worked against Lendl's powerful ground strokes. Against some opponents, Chang could count on the clay to sap some of that strength and even up the playing field. Not against Lendl, who had rallied from two sets down to beat John McEnroe in the French Open final in 1984.

Lendl also had won the first major of the year in Australia, taken 33 of 35 matches, and had five tournament titles in 1989 when he reached Paris. He fully expected to push deep into the Open.

And he was pushing aside Chang, winning the first two sets
6-4, 6-4.

"I felt very comfortable and in control, but then he began
playing better, maybe a little desperate," Lendl said.

Chang won the third and fourth sets by 6-3 scores. Momen-
tum was his. The crowd was his. A historic triumph could be
his if he completed the comeback.

Then the cramps hit. At times, Chang doubled over in pain.
He walked stiffly between points. He even thought about quit-
ting.

"He showed a lot of courage and deserves credit for it,"
Lendl said. "When you get cramps, it's very painful and it's almost impossible to play."

At times, Chang served underhand because he couldn't
stretch out in the normal serving manner. Indeed, his usual
serve wasn't much more than a lollypop anyway. He also resorted to a series of high lobs, called moonballs, to offset Lendl's power and to befuddle the Czech.

"I had to try something," Chang said. "I tried to break his
concentration. I was just popping in my serves any way I could.
I think the underhand serve shocked him a little."

Between points—each player has about 15 seconds to get
ready—he'd quickly swig some water. Between games (a minute or more is allowed), Chang drank and drank and drank,
getting as much water as possible, attempting to offset the signs
of dehydration. He didn't sit on the sideline, choosing to stand
rather than chance being completely overtaken by the cramps
and having to retire.

The knots in his legs were, at times, the size of tennis balls.
There was no way Chang could hang with Lendl physically in
the fifth set.

But Chang's strategy had unnerved Lendl, who began losing

patience, making unforced errors. Too eager to put away the staggering American, Lendl became increasingly frustrated.

Meanwhile, especially on Lendl's serves, Chang was going for outright winners. He had no choice.

"I was surprised I was able to hold on so long," Chang said. "When I was given a warning [for stalling], both my thighs were cramping. I thought I could no longer go on, but I said my prayers and the cramps went away a little. I tried to keep calm and not panic."

He didn't. Lendl did.

"It's difficult playing against someone with cramps," he added, "If it happens early in the match when you're still fresh, you can take advantage of the situation. But in the fifth set, after you've been playing for four hours, it's hard to accelerate the pace and make him run around. It's a lottery."

In this lottery, it was the mental aspect that allowed Chang to prevail.

Although his weak serve was broken twice by Lendl in the fifth set, Chang broke four times. On match point, sensing it was "now or never," Chang resorted to a tactic he'd used before, although never on such a grand stage. He positioned himself not behind the end line, as is normal, but just behind the service line. When Lendl looked up and saw his opponent inches behind the service box, he was stunned—and unable to adjust.

Lendl double-faulted, and Chang fell flat on his back. Not from pain, but from relief.

Final: Chang 6, Lendl 3! Just 17 years old and clearly not at his top physical form, Chang had remarkably whipped the No. 1 ranked player in the world.

"I would always play guys that were older than me," Chang said of his final-point strategy. "They would see this little squirt across the net and they would get a little nervous because of my age and my position behind the service box. I would never do that to insult them or make fun of them. When you are in a situation where you are desperate to win a point, you do anything to bother the concentration of the opponent."

It was the biggest victory of Chang's short pro career. He'd been the youngest ever to win a main-draw match at the U.S. Open at 15 years, 6 months. But this 4-hour, 38-minute drama was headline grabbing.

"I've been in tennis some years and this is the most incredible match I ever saw," said Jose Higueras, Chang's coach and a formidable clay-courter in his own right. "Mike showed he has the stuff of a champion. He's a very smart player. It was memorable."

And controversial.

"He doesn't do it for nothing," Haiti's Ronald Agenor, Chang's next foe, said of Chang's unusual style. "It's to unbalance the opponent. It bothers you. It's a mental attack as he forces you to think."

Added the outspoken McEnroe, who missed the 1989 French Open with a back injury:

"It's incredible that a teen-ager like Chang can beat the world's No. 1 player in Paris. I take offense at these little guys coming in and winning.

"If it happens every 10 years that's one thing, but they're getting away with murder. . . . The circuit's made for 17–21 year olds who have nothing on their minds except tennis. It's not made for 30-year-olds."

Chang felt like a 60-, no, an 80-year-old. And two days later, he had to face Agenor.

But at 17—McEnroe be damned—Chang's recuperative powers were superb. He was ready physically for Agenor, and he even used the same "crowding" maneuver on one of Agenor's critical serves in the fourth set. Chang beat Agenor 6-4, 2-6, 6-4, 7-6, becoming the youngest semifinalist in French Open history.

In defeat, Agenor was less gracious than Lendl.

"He wouldn't play that way at 2-2 in the first set, he only does it on important points," he said of Chang. "It's an intelligent move and he's an intelligent player, but he won't win Roland Garros that way."

Win Roland Garros? That thought barely entered Chang's mind when he came to Paris. Now, he was two victories away from doing precisely that.

"He's surprised everybody, even himself," tennis great Rod Laver said.

He needed to do some more surprising, though.

In the semifinals, Chang faced Russia's Andrei Chesnokov, another clay-court specialist. Again, Chang was plagued by cramps, albeit not as painfully as against Lendl. And again, Chang won in four sets, 6-1, 5-7, 7-6, 7-5, becoming the youngest finalist in a men's Grand Slam event.

"It's definitely a dream," Chang said after drawing a standing ovation from the 14,500 fans at center court. "It's something special I'll always have with me."

He could barely show his appreciation to the fans, though.

"I'm excited inside, but I'm a quiet person," Chang said. "It's hard to jump around when you're drained. You don't have any energy left to show excitement."

Whatever energy remained he needed to save for the final, against Sweden's Stefan Edberg, who already owned three major titles. Edberg, known for his prowess on faster surfaces, was on a roll at Roland Garros.

"A lot of people didn't think I could play on clay, but I've always thought I could," said Edberg, the No. 3 seed. "I've really put it together these last two weeks. I know how to play on clay now. I just have to be patient and play my own game."

Chang was aware that no American had won the French since Tony Trabert in 1955.

"I don't think about that sort of thing because it would put extra pressure on me," Chang said. "I just go out and give it my all. Whatever happens, happens."

What happened was the final chapter in one of tennis's most amazing upset runs.

From the beginning, Chang was on his game, using well-placed passing shots and an assortment of off-speed forays to win the first set 6-1. But Edberg simply had needed time to get warmed up, and when he did, he caught fire.

The Swede won the next two sets, 6-3 and 6-4. When he broke Chang's serve in the fourth set, the American kid's scintillating run seemed about to end.

Edberg held 10 break points in three games of that fourth set. Chang never faltered, winning each of those points by raising his game to yet another level. Each time Edberg came to the net, which was often, Chang found the right antidote: precise passing shots, deft lobs, and volleys.

Chang turned his two greatest allies, quickness and relentlessness, into indomitable forces.

"I thought the match was gone," Chang said. "A few points probably inspired me to try even harder and to believe there was a chance I could come back."

There was. And he did.

When Chang broke Edberg's serve at 5-4, he owned the fourth set. Although Chang immediately lost his serve to begin the final set, he was confident he could handle Edberg's services. He broke right back, surged to a 4-1 lead in the set, and sensed that Edberg was fading.

*Seventeen-year-old Michael Chang shocked the tennis world with his victory over Stefan Edberg in the final of the 1989 French Open.*

"In the fifth set I felt a little tired," admitted Edberg.

Chang kept coming, holding his serve for a 5-2 lead.

"He seldom misses," Edberg said. "He probably has one of the best passing shots in the game. He can hit them down the line or cross court. Because he's so quick, he has a lot of time to hit the ball."

When Edberg hit the ball into the net on the final point, a mighty roar emanated from the stands. The championship was Chang's, and he threw up his arms in victory before gesturing to Higueras and his family.

"It's a great honor and achievement. At the moment, it's the highest achievement I could ever have in tennis," Chang said. "These two weeks, regardless of what happened today, are going to stay with me throughout my whole life.

"Maybe some day I'll be able to achieve something greater. I don't want to dwell on this victory. I don't want to limit myself. I want to be able to keep on going and do even better."

Among the most excited observers was Trabert, who was providing television commentary for Chang's momentous win.

"I'm really happy for him," Trabert said. "I thought he played extremely well. I didn't have anything to do with it, but every year I get calls around the time of the French asking me if any American will do it. At least that's over now.

"I thought if anybody had a chance it would be Andre Agassi, but I didn't think he could do it physically. I certainly didn't think Michael would win it at the beginning of the tournament."

So why did it happen?

"The thing about Michael is he takes risks when he's under pressure," Trabert said. "He gambles instead of playing it safe. To produce under pressure the way he did is something else. He has a lot of courage.

"Lots of Americans become defensive on the [clay] surface.

They don't make anything happen. You've got to make things happen in this game."

Added Edberg: "He's played a lot of tough matches and he kept coming back all the time. You have to admire him for that. He's young. Maybe he doesn't think about it that much."

Chang wasn't the only teenager to win the 1989 French. Spain's bubbly Arantxa Sanchez took the women's crown.

"It's the changing of the guard," said Philippe Chatrier, president of the International Tennis Federation. "The fact we've had two 17-year-old winners is unique for Roland Garros and the Grand Slam.

"These two victories show that tennis is far from stagnant as everybody has been saying. A page has been turned and the young are taking power."

Not quite in Chang's case. Although he would reach No. 2 in the world during his career, Chang never won another Grand Slam title. He didn't make the final of a major until the 1995 French, when he lost to Thomas Muster. In 1996, he lost to Boris Becker in the Australian Open championship match. The same year, he was beaten by Pete Sampras in the U.S. Open final.

In 1992, in a rematch with Edberg, Chang lost the longest French Open match, a 5-hour, 26-minute marathon in the semifinals.

Chang did make a mark in Davis Cup play, helping lead the United States to the championship in 1990 after recovering from a broken hip, one of many injuries that would wear on him. He rallied from two sets down in the decisive semifinal match against Austria in Vienna, fighting off leg cramps and the vociferous crowd to beat Horst Skoff. It was the first time in 53 years that an American came from 0-2 in sets in the fifth match of a Davis Cup series and won.

He then won both of his matches against Australia, lifting the Americans to the most prestigious team title in tennis.

"It's unique in the game of tennis," Chang said of the Davis Cup. "You can't really compare it to playing in a regular tournament, because now you're representing your team and playing for your country. The crowds are more vocal and the atmosphere is a bit more exciting."

While Chang remained an exciting player whose grit and speed made him a crowd favorite, he never again reached the heights of his only Grand Slam victory. When he retired in 2004, he'd played in more Grand Slam tournaments (57) than anyone but Jimmy Connors.

He'd also become a spokesman for his strong religious beliefs and for civil liberties. As an American of Chinese descent, Chang often offered his views on his heritage and the plight of people in China.

"I'll look at some of the pictures of what happened in Tiananmen Square and, coming from an Asian background and being Chinese, it hurts a little bit," Chang told the Associated Press in 1990 during his French Open title defense. "Between what happened here [in Paris] and what happened in Beijing, it made me want to fight harder."

Fighting hard never was a problem for Michael Chang.

# 18

## THE GREATEST SUBDUES THE BEAR

He was the golden boy from the Olympics, someone to idolize for representing his country so valiantly and successfully in the ring at Rome.

Or he was the brash loudmouth boxer from Kentucky, the Louisville Lip, who needed to get his lights dimmed and his tongue silenced.

Your view of Cassius Clay pretty much depended on such things as politics, race, patriotism, and bombast. One thing was certain as he prepared for the biggest bout of his young life: There was no way you could ignore him.

Of course, that would never change as Clay would become one of the most significant people, athlete or otherwise, of the 20th century. As Muhammad Ali, his effect on the world carried well beyond the squared circle, and at one point, he accurately pointed out that he was "the most recognized person on the planet."

"And," he added with that mischievous smile, "the prettiest."

Early on, though, he was simply Cassius Marcellus Clay, boxer.

In 1960, Clay won a gold medal at the Rome Games. He turned pro soon after that and swiftly made his way through hand-chosen opponents for more than a year.

In 1962, the boxers in the other corner were a bit more accomplished, and by the end of the year, Clay had knocked out former champion Archie Moore, a legend in the sport.

After three convincing wins in 1963, Clay had risen to the top of the heavyweight rankings, the No. 1 contender to face the fearsome champion, Sonny Liston, for the most prized crown in professional sports at the time.

Ah, Liston. Charles "Sonny" Liston, who had destroyed the popular Floyd Patterson in one round to take the heavyweight title, then knocked out Patterson in one round again to keep it.

Liston's image, much of it created by a media disappointed with his total lack of glamour, suffered in comparison to Patterson. And, of course, to Clay.

Not that Liston complained when he was called "an animal in the ring" by opponents. Or that newspapermen dubbed him a brute. Liston, who would serve time in prison and who was linked to mobsters throughout his career, believed strongly in the powers of intimidation.

Liston ran away from home at age 13 to escape abject poverty and the beatings of a tyrannical father. He found himself drawn to the violence of the sport of boxing. He did not find himself drawn to the rantings of Clay.

Indeed, he was so turned off by Clay that when told the odds on the fight were 7-to-1, Liston not only laughed loudly but also allegedly went looking for bookmakers who would handle his own bet on the fight. Liston believed the odds would have been 50-to-1 or higher if a champion more respected by the public and the press—a Rocky Marciano, a Joe Louis—held the title and was facing a clown such as Clay.

David Neal, who 25 years later would produce an NBC television special about the fight, was just 8 years old on February 25, 1964, the night of the title bout. He, like many others in the latter years of the 20th century, at first had no clue about the circumstances of the fight.

"I knew it was the first of two fights between Clay and Liston, and that it went longer than the second one," he said. "I also knew it was the last time Ali fought as Cassius Clay. But I had no idea how monumental an upset it was. I had thought Liston was just a stepping stone for Ali."

Not quite.

"To say Liston was the [Mike] Tyson of his day is to understate it," said Dr. Ferdie Pacheco, who worked Clay's corner for many of his fights, including the Miami Beach meeting with Liston. "Everybody they put in front of him, he knocked out. It didn't seem like there was a human being on earth who could beat him."

Clay knew better. He was not only a gifted boxer with a precise jab, superb body control, and speed more fitting of a lightweight, but he was also smart. There are those who argue that Clay/Ali was the most intellectual fighter ever.

He brilliantly used that intellect outside the ring, too. Clay, who had embraced Islam and soon, as Muhammad Ali, would loudly and proudly proclaim himself as a Black Muslim, undertook a one-man verbal campaign to unnerve the nerveless champion. While previous opponents paid their homage to Liston's might and power, Clay disparaged him with a torrent of insults.

Many said Clay was wasting his breath, that Liston's resolve was unshakable, his armor impenetrable. But Cassius Clay/Muhammad Ali rarely wasted his words.

Clay insulted Liston at every opportunity during the buildup to the bout. He called the champion "a big, ugly bear," then ridiculed Liston's lack of education. He began talking about what he would do once he was champion, once he'd "whupped" Liston into submission. Clay liked to predict the rounds in which fights would end; Liston would go in eight, he said.

And he even wrote poetry.

Yes, a boxer who favored rhymes. Such as this piece of advice:

> Everyone knew when I stepped in town, I was the greatest fighter around.
> A lot of people called me a clown, but I am the one who called the round.
> The people came to see a great fight, but all I did was put out the light.
> Never put your money against Cassius Clay, for you will never have a lucky day.

And this bit of prose about what would happen when he and Liston stepped into the ring:

> Now Clay swings with a right, what a beautiful swing.
> And the punch raises the Bear clear of the ring.
> Liston is still rising, and the ref wears a frown.
> For he can't start counting, till Sonny comes down.
> Now Liston disappears from view.
> The crowd is getting frantic,
> But our radar stations have picked him up.
> He's somewhere over the Atlantic.
> Who would have thought when they came to the fight

That they'd witness the launching of a human satellite.
Yes, the crowd did not dream when they lay down their money
That they would see a total eclipse of the Sonny.
I am the greatest.

At least in his own opinion he was No. 1. But Clay had to prove it all in the ring, and there were very few who shared his viewpoint.

Perhaps even fewer shared it after the weigh-in.

In one of the more bizarre scenes in the theater of the absurd that is boxing, Clay began yelling, pointing, basically throwing a fit. He appeared to be hysterical with fear.

"People said he's going to freeze, that he's so scared he's going to drop dead," reported Murray Rose of the Associated Press.

Others shared the opinion.

"Liston was . . . an intimidator who knocked people out," said boxing historian Bert Sugar. "Clay acted so crazy at the weigh-in that the doctors wanted to cancel the fight. He was fast and he was brash, but hardly anybody gave him a chance against Liston."

Added Pacheco: "His blood pressure was 220 over 120. At 220, the top of your head should be blowing off.

"He wanted to convince Liston that he was fighting a lunatic," the ring doc added, "because a bully doesn't know what to do with a crazy man."

Clay was convincing, so much so that Liston himself dubbed his opponent "a crazy kid." But, tellingly, Liston also had once confided that he was afraid of no one except "crazy men who could do anything for no reason."

Clay's act at the weigh-in had the desired effect. Although the challenger was completely calm just a few minutes later, the champion was befuddled. Just what was this madman capable of?

For almost certainly the first time in his career, Liston carried some doubts into the ring. And that's all Clay felt he needed.

Clay wore into the ring a robe with "The Lip" embroidered on the back in red letters. As both fighters took their instructions at the center of the ring, Clay looked directly into Liston's glare and said, "Now I've got you, Chump."

Not Champ. Chump.

Then he went about getting Liston.

Clay knew that Liston would want an early knockout, just as he'd done to the unfortunate Patterson, who entered their two fights fearing for his own safety and thus had no chance. He knew that Liston would throw rights, lefts, hooks, uppercuts, haymakers—anything to get rid of this "crazy kid."

And Clay also knew that if he remained smart and true to his game plan, Liston wouldn't hurt him.

Staying away from the potent punches Liston unleashed, Clay danced. He bounced off the ropes before Liston could trap him. And while the champ did land some vicious shots, he was able to make only partial contact with Clay, never hurting the challenger.

Clay, in fact, didn't do a whole lot of fighting in the first two rounds. He did plenty of frustrating, though.

"He didn't know what was going on," Clay said. "He couldn't believe I was still standing."

Not just standing: In the third round, Clay took the fight to Liston, sticking and moving, feinting and flurrying. Landing swift combinations, then moving away only to come at Liston from another angle and do more damage, Clay clearly was in charge.

And Liston got cut, the ultimate indignation for a man who considered himself untouchable.

In his corner before the fourth round, Liston's handlers applied a balm to close the wound. Suspicious observers claim they also put the gel on his gloves, and when he threw punches at Clay, the liniment—nobody ever determined exactly what it was—flew into Clay's eyes.

After Round 4, which Clay controlled for nearly the entire three minutes, the challenger was in panic mode as he returned to his corner.

"I can't see, I'm blind," Clay screamed. "Cut off the gloves, cut 'em off!"

His trainer, Angelo Dundee, had no intention of letting Clay quit a fight he was ready to win.

"In a pig's eye," Dundee said. "This is for the big apple."

Dundee soaked Clay's eyes with a sponge, hoping to wash out the substance; it was the only remedy his fighter really needed.

"A couple of guys down below were yelling at me and cursing me out. They thought I'd done something," Dundee said.

So his brother, Jimmy, ran to the corner and told him "to put the sponge in your eyes and show them there's nothing wrong with the water." Angelo did so, quieting the protesters.

"It could have been two things that blurred his vision—liniment from Liston's shoulder or Monsel's solution [a coagulant used to treat cuts]," Dundee said. "We took care of it."

Pacheco credits Dundee for keeping the great upset going.

"Angelo saved Ali's crown," Pacheco said. "If he doesn't send him out for the fifth round, the fight is over."

Clay's vision cleared somewhat, but Liston had sensed vulnerability. Incensed by being cut, as well, he went for the knockout while Clay tried to stay away until he had full use of his eyes.

Liston's marksmanship was poor—or maybe Clay's survival instincts were too sharp. Never did the champ land a punch capable of producing a knockout in the fifth, and by the end of the round Clay again was in charge.

This time for good.

"I knew Ali had the fight won after he made it through the fifth round," Pacheco said. "Liston hit him with everything he

*Cassius Clay—soon to change his name to Muhammad Ali— following his victory over Sonny Liston in 1964.*

had, the kind of shots that knocked everyone else out, but they didn't have any effect on Ali."

They had plenty effect on Liston, who rarely had gone so long in his bouts. His plodding style, in comparison to his "float like a butterfly" opponent, left him few resources once he began to tire.

"All the time we were looking for the big punch from Liston," said the AP's Rose.

It wasn't coming from the spent champion.

Who knows what Liston's mental outlook could have been in that sixth round, but he appeared to be a beaten man. Clay did all the damage, and when Liston struggled back to his stool, he had nothing left.

The bell sounded for Round 7, but Liston never budged from his stool. Citing a damaged shoulder, he quit.

Pandemonium. Clay jumped into his handlers' arms, raising his gloves, kicking out his legs, bouncing around the ring. And talking, naturally.

He shouted to reporters at ringside: "Don't you go saying this was no fix."

No, that would wait for the rematch, when Liston would go down and out in the first round on a punch that almost nobody saw—the so-called phantom punch.

After the Miami fight, Clay officially changed from his "slave name" to his Muslim moniker, Muhammad Ali. He was headed for one of the most significant careers in sports history. From Islam icon to leader of his race. From draft protester to symbol of political freedom. From loudmouth to legend.

"Ali changed the perception of what a sports hero was," Pacheco reasoned. "Back then, sports heroes had to be self-effacing, 'aw-shucks' kind of guys. Now here was a guy who told everybody he was the greatest and backed it up. But he did it with such spontaneity and childlike glee that people accepted it."

# 19

## FASTER THAN A SPEEDING BULLET

In the spring of 1995, it was business as usual at the Oakland airport. So many people coming and going, including one group of men that stuck out from the others because of their size.

They were members of the Golden State Warriors, in town for the 20th anniversary of their NBA championship season of 1974–1975.

It was quite a different scene from the one that greeted them in the spring of 1975 after winning the title.

There had been so many people in the landing area that day that their plane was forced to reroute to San Francisco. The players then used ground transportation to get them to the Oakland airport.

"I remember this incredible crush of people," said Warriors star Rick Barry. "We got really scared because they caved in the roof of the cab we were in."

The fans' fervor could be justified. After all, the Warriors had just surprised the Washington Bullets in the NBA finals for their first championship. No, make that shocked them.

The Warriors were not given much of a chance to win the championship, particularly with the East Division's longtime domination of the West (17 of the previous 20 titles).

The Boston Celtics had won most of those, but the defending champions were eliminated by the Bullets in six games in 1975.

The Bullets kept pretty much the same team for three seasons and were considered the most talented squad in the NBA. The Warriors had only one starter back from the previous year.

So what did Golden State do? Merely take four straight from the Bullets, who had the league's best record along with the Celtics (60-22) in 1974–1975 and had won three of four from the Warriors during the regular season.

"It was like a fairy-tale season," Barry said. "Everything just fell into place."

Barry called it the greatest upset in NBA Finals history.

Indeed.

The Bullets were led by superstars Elvin Hayes and Wes Unseld, two of the top frontcourt players in the game, and sharpshooting Phil Chenier.

The Warriors had only one bona fide star in Barry and mostly a cast of role-players that included a center by committee.

"I guess no one took us very seriously," Warriors coach Al Attles said.

Nope. Attles was watching TV in his hotel room prior to the finals when he heard one newscaster say, "The Warriors are the worst team to be in the championship series in the history of the league."

"I was so mad, I was about to throw something at the TV," Attles said. "But I didn't because I knew I'd have to pay for it."

That particular newscaster wasn't the only one who had a poor opinion of the Warriors, who had won but 48 games and lost 34 during a mediocre year. Going back to the start of the season, the Bullets were pretty much set with their lineup of Hayes, Unseld, Chenier, playmaker Kevin Porter, and Mike Riordan, a hard-nosed player known for his tough defense. Not so the Warriors, who had question marks at center and at one of the forward positions opposite Barry.

Strapped for cash, the Warriors had traded veteran center Nate Thurmond to the Chicago Bulls. In return they received Clifford Ray, a draft choice, and $500,000. Although Thurmond was nearing the end of a brilliant career, the move for Ray didn't exactly encourage enthusiasm among the Warriors' followers.

The 6-foot-9 Ray was considered a journeyman center who would never star in the NBA. Another factor: Ray had undergone major knee surgery just two years before.

George Johnson, a pencil-thin center from Dillard College, shared a good portion of the frontcourt load as a backup to Ray. Johnson was still an unknown quantity, and the same could be said for rookie Jamaal Wilkes.

Wilkes, a controversial first-round draft pick by the Warriors, was expected to be no more than a backup at small forward behind Barry. At 6-foot-6 and 190 pounds, he looked the part.

All of a sudden Wilkes found himself starting at power forward opposite Barry when forwards Cazzie Russell and Clyde Lee moved to other clubs before the season started. Wilkes's primary job was now rebounding as well as scoring, mixing it up under the boards with the league's biggest players.

"There were a lot of questions about whether I could survive the rigors of the NBA," Wilkes admitted.

Wilkes did enjoy playing alongside Barry, a one-man scoring machine who never met a hoop rim he didn't like. Barry could roll up 20 points even on a bad shooting night. On a good night, he could go for 30 to 40. He was second to none as a foul shooter, having created a near-perfect technique with his archaic underhand motion. Barry once went through an entire season with only nine misses at the free throw line, and when he retired he held the all-time NBA percentage mark with .900 for his career.

Barry could also thread his passes through a needle and often set up teammates for easy shots. He was Larry Bird before there was a Larry Bird.

"You learn a lot from Barry just watching him," Wilkes said.

Barry's hotly competitive nature didn't win him many friends in the league, though. Nor did his swaggering self-confidence that bordered on arrogance.

"I was not an easy person to get along with," Barry admitted in later years. "I didn't have a lot of tact."

Barry, a New Jersey native, won an NCAA scoring championship with the University of Miami. He later won an NBA scoring title with the San Francisco Warriors, bettering the great Oscar Robertson by five points a game. Barry would later win another scoring championship in the upstart American Basketball Association, becoming the first player to win an NCAA scoring crown and scoring titles in two professional leagues. However, he was mostly remembered for the controversy surrounding his jump to the fledgling ABA.

Barry was the biggest NBA name to cross over when he decided to join the Oakland Oaks, creating instant credibility for the new league. His own image was suffering, however. The San Francisco Warriors took Barry to court in an attempt to stop the move. They argued that he still had an obligation to fulfill his contract with them. The court dispute sidelined Barry for the entire 1967–1968 season before he was allowed to join the Oaks. He made an immediate impact, leading them to the ABA championship.

A couple of ABA teams and another court decision later, Barry was back in the NBA with the Warriors—now called Golden State—for the 1972–1973 season.

Barry's ABA adventure wasn't the easiest of times for him. But he came back to the NBA a better all-around player. Asked about the experience of jumping leagues, Barry noted: "If I had to do it all over again, I would wait for some other fool to do it."

With the Warriors, Barry picked up right where he left off. He was the golden boy for Golden State, the complete offensive focus of his team. Barry continued to raise his game, and during the 1974–1975 season, he averaged 30.6 points to finish as the No. 2 scorer in the NBA.

The Warriors usually went as Barry went. And against the Chicago Bulls in the seventh game of the Western finals, they didn't seem to be going anywhere. Barry was struggling as the Warriors fell behind by 14 points late in the second quarter. At the half, the usually sharp-shooting Barry had managed to make only 2 of his 15 shots.

He spent much of the third period on the bench, but then he started connecting. Aided by a strong performance by Wilkes, the NBA's surprise rookie of the year, the Warriors rallied to pull out an 83-79 victory and move into the finals.

The Bullets, after they'd eliminated the Celtics, were completely focused on stopping Barry in the finals—and they had the stopper to do it in Riordan.

During the season, the Bullets held Barry to 20.8 points a game, nearly 10 points under his average. The main reason was Riordan, who shut down Barry's production to 8 points in one game and 12 in another. In three games against Riordan, Barry managed to average only 16.3 points. In the one game that Riordan didn't play against the Warriors, Barry scored 34.

Guess who was guarding Barry in the finals.

"I guess Barry had some off-nights with his shooting," Attles said, "but it's still unusual for a big scorer to be held down like that. Mike really stays with the man he's guarding."

Sometimes a little too close for Attles's taste. This would spark a violent episode in Game 4 of the series.

First, though, the Warriors seemed out of rhythm in the opening game when they fell behind by 14 points in the first half. Perhaps, as one writer suggested, the Warriors were suffering from jet lag after their flight to the east from the west coast. When the starters continued to struggle after intermission, falling behind by 16 in the third period, Attles sent in his reserves. Derrek Dickey, Charles Dudley, and Phil Smith made key contributions as Golden State rallied for a 101-95 victory.

"Things will be different," Unseld predicted.

They were. The Warriors usually played their home games in the Oakland Coliseum, but the arena had been booked for the Ice Follies during the time of the NBA Finals—no doubt because of the unlikelihood of the Warriors needing it at that time. The series was forced to move to the Cow Palace in San Francisco for Games 2 and 3.

The Warriors hadn't played a home game there in four years, and only a handful of their players had ever played there at all. But Attles didn't see it as a big problem.

"It's not the arena but the crowd that gives you the home-court advantage," Attles said, "and we'll have it."

But for a while, it didn't seem to be too much of an advantage for the Warriors. They fell behind early and trailed by 13 points on four occasions in the second quarter.

Once again they rallied, this time behind the hot-shooting

*The Golden State Warriors, 1975 NBA champions.*

Barry. He capped a 36-point performance with two free throws with 23 seconds remaining to spark an exciting 92-91 victory for Golden State.

"Our team seems to play its best basketball when we're down," Barry said. "We thrive on adversity."

Barry had to be thinking about the semifinal series against Chicago. The Warriors, down three games to two and all but counted out, won a game on the road and then another at home to clinch a berth in the finals. Both times they rallied from big deficits.

Barry could have done with a little less adversity against the powerful Bullets, though.

"I would like to see us get ahead by 13 points this time," Barry said, looking ahead to Game 3 at the Cow Palace.

Barry got his wish—sort of. The Warriors led from the start and never trailed by more than 2 (56-54 early in the second quarter). Then they started steamrolling the Bullets behind Barry's slick shooting. With about five minutes left in the game, the Warriors removed all but one of their regulars and finished with a solid 109-101 victory behind Barry's 38 points.

With a 3-0 lead in the best-of-seven series, the Warriors were on the verge of the unthinkable: a four-game sweep of the best team in the league.

It had been a total team effort for the Warriors, who used every one of their 12 athletic players to wear down the Bullets. Barry led the way with his scoring, passing, and leadership ability.

"I've never seen anyone more involved in the team concept of basketball," said Warriors rookie guard Phil Smith, answering critics that Barry was a selfish player. "Everything he does is for the team, not Rick Barry, and that's why we're where we are right now."

It was desperation time for the Bullets. More to the point: desperation time for Mike Riordan.

In the fourth game, Riordan went all out to stop Barry. Attles thought he went too far when he put a headlock on his star player early in the game. The coach rushed out to defend Barry, only to be ejected.

"It was nice to have Al behind me," Barry said. "He's tough. As for Riordan, I guess he thought he was playing rugby."

Riordan had been pestering Barry from the opening tip-off, according to Attles, trying to draw him into a fight so that both could get thrown out. The Bullets would get the better of the deal.

"He didn't even go for the ball," Attles said after watching Riordan take a swing at Barry.

Attles went back to the dressing room and watched the rest of the game on a television set. This is what he saw:

The Warriors fell behind by 14 points before making a comeback.

"We just went chip, chip, chip away when they were 14 ahead," Barry said, "and I think the Bullets were looking over their shoulder, looking for us to catch up again."

The Warriors did. Then Golden State fell behind by 8 points in the last five minutes, but the team caught the Bullets again with the help of crucial Washington turnovers.

With 1:55 remaining, Hayes made one of two free throws to give Washington a 93-92 lead.

With 1:45 left, Butch Beard knifed in for a layup to put the Warriors ahead 94-93.

Then with 86 seconds left, Unseld threw the ball away.

"We pressured the ball," said Joe Roberts, who had replaced Attles as coach. "We pressured their big men . . . men who aren't used to handling the ball."

With 33 seconds left, Washington had another chance to take the lead, but Unseld turned the ball over after taking Chenier's pass from out of bounds.

There were 19 seconds remaining when Beard was fouled. He made one of two free throws to give the Warriors a 95-93 lead.

Still plenty of time for the Bullets to come back. But Beard was fouled by Hayes with 9 seconds left while rebounding a shot by Chenier. Beard had to make only one of three shots to wrap up the game for the Warriors; there was no NBA three-point shot in those days. He missed the first. Then he missed the second.

On his third attempt, the ball finally dropped through the hoop. It gave the Warriors a three-point lead, enough to withstand a late basket by Unseld.

Final: Golden State 96, Washington 95.

The Warriors were NBA champions!

And they had won the title in the most unlikely fashion possible, a sweep that included two victories on the Bullets' home court.

In the locker room, a champagne-drenched Barry smoked a victory cigar and tried to find the words to express his feelings. He found many.

"Incredible . . . unfathomable . . . unreal . . . amazing."

For one remarkable playoff run, the Golden State Warriors deserved every one of those adjectives.

# 20

## NEW ENGLAND'S
## SUPER BOWL STUNNER

The NFL's strangest season just had to end with one of its most unexpected champions.

In 2001, when everything in America changed on a cloudless Tuesday in September, America turned to sports as much for relief as for entertainment. Football fans were energized by the long shot that came in: the New England Patriots.

As we've subsequently learned, this franchise has been masterfully built, has been brilliantly coached, and has turned into one of the great teams in NFL annals. But the 2001 Patriots had no business being a contender, let alone a champion. And beating the offensive juggernaut St. Louis Rams in the Super Bowl? Forget that.

New England's season began much like the previous one, the first under Bill Belichick, when the Pats finished 5-11 and the folks from Boston to Hartford, Manchester to Bangor, considered the new coach a poor imitation of his mentor, Bill Parcells. The Patriots lost their opener at Cincinnati 23–17.

Two days later, still smarting from a defeat against such a perennial doormat as the Bengals, the team's coaching staff was beginning preparations for the Carolina Panthers when the World Trade Center and the Pentagon were attacked by terrorists. Even the tunnel vision of NFL coaches was infiltrated by those heinous acts and their aftermath.

Belichick, whose father had coached at the Naval Academy, was one of the more perceptive members of the NFL coaching fraternity when addressing the issues facing not only his team and his sport but also Americans everywhere.

Uncertain whether the NFL would stage its games on the upcoming weekend, Belichick recalled 1963, when President John F. Kennedy was assassinated but the games went on. Pete Rozelle, then the NFL's commissioner, admitted afterward it was the decision he most regretted making in his career.

"It was really a pretty emotional week," said Belichick, who was going through a similar week in 2001. "The decision was made not to postpone the game for a week and still play it. But that's one of those things that when you live through it, you not only don't ever forget the event, but you don't ever forget the impact."

And what about the impact of September 11? Should current commissioner Paul Tagliabue postpone the games?

Belichick understood both sides of the issue. On the one hand, it was about not letting terrorists disrupt normal life in America.

"On the other hand," Belichick said, "you're talking about a pretty significant tragedy here and I think that needs to be respected."

And it was. The games were moved to the first weekend in January, when the playoffs were supposed to begin. That called for significant adjustments to the overall schedule, including pushing the Super Bowl back one week to February.

But it was necessary.

"It would have been really hard to play," said Patriots starting guard Joe Andruzzi, whose two brothers helped clear the rubble and look for survivors at the World Trade Center.

It wasn't much easier getting ready to return.

"I don't want to say business as usual, because there definitely is a different tone here this week," linebacker Ted Johnson said as the Patriots got ready to face the division rival New York Jets. "So far, I think everybody seems to be tuned in to what's going on and their jobs. We've got a long week this week, so that will benefit us in that sense. Compared to last week, it's like night and day. Our attention is much clearer and much more focused than it was last week at this time.

"Playing this weekend is appropriate, whereas last weekend, I thought that we were still pretty raw from our emotions as a nation. This weekend, I think it will be a welcome sight to see football games."

The players and coaches knew they'd sense a difference, though. They simply couldn't let thoughts of what was happening around them infiltrate their concentration on their assignments.

"It's like anything else," Belichick said. "It's there, you're aware of it, but you're more aware of what the job is at hand and what you can actually control and do something about. You have to have confidence in everybody else that they're taking care of their end of the security and the logistics of the event."

Before the game at Gillette Stadium—and before each NFL game that weekend—ceremonies remembered the victims and paid tribute to the military and the police and fire departments. It was a tearful, respectful time, and the presence of as many

American flags as you'd expect to see at an Independence Day parade was, somehow, comforting.

"It was Americans showing their pride," said Jets coach Herman Edwards, "and it made me proud."

In the game itself, both teams appeared distracted, rusty.

The Jets won 10-3, sinking the Patriots to 0-2 and putting their playoff hopes in dire straits before September was over. Even worse, New England lost veteran quarterback Drew Bledsoe.

While scrambling toward the sideline late in the game, Bledsoe was hit (cleanly, but viciously) by linebacker Mo Lewis. The impact sent Bledsoe sprawling, and he was dazed when he got up. He returned for one series but really was in no condition to continue, and the next day, doctors determined Bledsoe had suffered internal bleeding.

For the foreseeable future, when they desperately needed to start winning, the Patriots would be without their offensive leader. The replacement: an untested second-year player from Michigan, a sixth-round draft pick named Tom Brady. The previous season, as a third-stringer, he completed one of three passes.

"I've always told myself to be ready for the opportunity, because you never know how many you're going to get," Brady said. "I'm ready to go. This is what you prepare for. You don't sit on an active roster to never expect to play. If that's the way I thought, I would never be here in the first place."

Brady's teammates weren't all that concerned about the emergency switch at the most important position on offense. In fact, they expected as much from the youngster as the veteran Bledsoe might provide.

"When I first got here I thought, if you didn't know Bledsoe was the man, you would think this was Brady's team," said receiver David Patten. "That's the type of confidence he brings."

"Tom's been around," added Troy Brown, who was drafted in 1993, the same year as Bledsoe. "Tom's really a confident person already. He's outspoken and he has true leadership ability."

Brady needed to push aside his feelings for the injured quarterback and concentrate on how he could get the Patriots into the victory column.

"It's hard to be overly excited from my standpoint just because he's a friend that's in the hospital," Brady said. "You don't get excited about something like that."

Patriots fans weren't exactly energized by the situation, either. With their team 0-2 and a totally green quarterback leading the offense, any optimism entering the season—and there wasn't a whole bunch of it, anyway—had dissipated.

That mood did not infiltrate the New England locker room, however. The taskmaster Belichick and his coordinators, Romeo Crennel on defense and Charlie Weis on offense, made certain of it.

But the next opponent was Indianapolis, which merely had scored the most points in the first two weeks of the season and was led by the nonpareil offensive trio of quarterback Peyton Manning, running back Edgerrin James, and wide receiver Marvin Harrison.

Yet it was the Patriots who blitzed the end zone in a 44-13 romp. They led 20-0 at halftime, returned two interceptions for touchdowns, and ran the ball as if the Colts' defense wasn't on the field, gaining 177 yards on the ground. That made it easy for Brady to manage the game, even though he was sacked on his first play.

"You envision the things that are going to happen in a game, all the possibilities," he said. "Never did I think it would be the runaway victory that it was."

So the Patriots were on their way? Not quite.

"Nobody thinks we're a good team right now, and we haven't proven it," cornerback Ty Law said. "But we won a game against a great team, and now we'll see if we can take it to Miami."

Instead, they took it on the chin at Miami, 30-10.

"To perform like this, there's just no excuse," Brady said after he threw for only 86 yards and fumbled a snap that defensive end Jason Taylor scored on. New England had three turnovers and allowed four sacks.

Now in a dire situation, the Patriots could have begun doubting themselves. They had the easy excuses:

◆ Playing in a difficult division
◆ Ravaged by injuries
◆ Disrupted by a suspension to veteran receiver Terry Glenn for violating the league's substance abuse policy, then Glenn's complaints about his signing bonus being withheld, even as he sat out with a hamstring injury
◆ No winning tradition under Belichick, who had flopped big-time in Cleveland in his previous head coaching job

An overtime victory the next week against San Diego got the Patriots thinking differently.

Trailing by 10 points with four minutes remaining, they staged a scintillating comeback that began their overall turnaround.

On New England's last two series in regulation, Adam Vinatieri's 23-yard field goal pulled the Pats to within 7, then a 3-yard touchdown pass from Brady to Jermaine Wiggins tied the game with 32 seconds left. In overtime, after San Diego punted, a 37-yard pass interference penalty set up Vinatieri's decisive 44-yard field goal.

Brady was sensational in a very tough spot; he had to throw

on almost every down in the fourth quarter. He completed 33 of 54 passes for 364 yards, all career bests by far.

"I've had a lot of games in college that came down to the same situation," he said. "I sure hope there's bigger days ahead in bigger arenas."

There would be, Tom. Many times.

New England won 38-17 at Indianapolis in its next game, and after a misstep at Denver, the Pats won two of their next three. At Thanksgiving, they stood at .500. Respectable, but hardly championship caliber.

"We're 5-5," Belichick said. "We have a third of the season left and we need to win and we need to win right now."

His players were listening. The Patriots reeled off victories against the Saints, Jets, Browns, and Bills. At 9-5, they were in the thick of the AFC East race as they prepared to host the archrival Dolphins, who led the division at 9-4.

A win would not only elevate the Patriots to the top of the division but also, with a combination of other results, give them a playoff spot. They would still have their bye week approaching before a final game against weak Carolina.

It also would be the last regular-season game at the deteriorating Foxboro Stadium, and what better way to bid adieu than to head into the postseason by knocking off Miami?

"After each win, it just gets more and more exciting," safety Lawyer Milloy said. "You evolve as a team and you make each situation, each game, that much more grand."

With Brady coming off a not-so-grand game in a 12-9 win at Buffalo, there was speculation a now-healthy Bledsoe might be reinserted at quarterback. The ever-charming Belichick merely responded with a brusque: "Nothing has changed."

And nothing had changed about the team's winning ways, either. The Patriots won 20-13, and although they didn't secure a division crown or playoff berth with the victory, it was special: They took several victory laps around the stadium, slap-ping hands with fans, paying tribute to those who had stuck with them.

"It'll be 10 minutes I won't ever forget for the rest of my life," linebacker Tedy Bruschi said.

One day later, when Seattle lost, the Patriots had that play-off spot. When they beat Carolina to conclude the season 11-5 (and on a six-game winning streak), they earned a bye for the first weekend of the playoffs, then a home game.

"When you are 1-3, that is a quarter of the season right there and you can't wait too long to make a move," Belichick said, recalling the Patriots' comeback from their slow start. "Being down by 10 points and rallying and coming back to win in overtime [against San Diego], that was certainly a critical game. But you can just keep going right down the line. When you are climbing uphill like that, every ledge is a big ledge to get to."

The ledge would get more slippery—downright icy—in the Patriots' next game.

Thanks to the geniuses at CBS and in the NFL's scheduling department, the second-round playoff game would be played on a Saturday night in Foxboro. In January. As if on cue, Mother Nature dumped snow (and more snow) on the field, causing whiteout conditions at times.

With Oakland as their opponent, the Pats already had a sig-nificant edge: The Raiders don't travel well in the cold and hadn't won a postseason game at a cold-weather site since 1981.

Yet it was the Raiders who led 13-10 in the final minutes. The Patriots were threatening, though, and Brady slipped, uh, dropped back to pass with 1:43 remaining. But the ball fell from his hand, Raiders linebacker Greg Biekert recovered, and it was ruled a fumble.

Game over. Season over.

Not quite.

The play was called for a replay review by officials in the replay booth. Belichick had his offense remain on the field, reasoning that Brady was attempting to tuck the ball in rather than throw it, and his arm was coming forward in that motion, making it an incomplete pass. The Raiders, already celebrating their upcoming trip to the AFC championship game, saw no validity to that claim.

Referee Walt Coleman took a long, thorough look at the replay, then ruled in the Pats' favor, citing the "tuck rule" that would forever become a beloved phrase in New England.

Vinatieri's line-drive 45-yard field goal off the snow-covered field and through the eerie, gray night tied it with 27 seconds remaining. He hit a 23-yarder in overtime to win it. Or steal it, depending on your viewpoint.

"Yeah, I was throwing the ball," a smiling Brady said. "How do you like that?"

The Raiders, of course, didn't like it one bit. They didn't have many kind words for Coleman, the rest of the officiating crew, the league itself, and of course, the Patriots.

"He pumped the ball, brought it back down. Maybe he wanted to bring it back up. Ball came out, game over," Raiders cornerback Charles Woodson said. "It kind of took the air out of a lot of guys. We knew the game was over. We were celebrating."

Prematurely, of course.

New England's magic journey next took the team to Pittsburgh. A win there meant an out-of-nowhere berth in the Super Bowl.

The Steelers were nine-point favorites after going 13-3 during the season and beating Baltimore, the defending NFL champion, in the playoffs. But Pittsburgh also had fallen short several times in AFC title games at home.

And the Patriots seemed as if they were charmed.

"Nobody can explain how we're doing it," said Johnson. "I know I can't put it into words."

The words coming from the Steelers weren't exactly reverential.

"We know very little about these guys," said star receiver Hines Ward. "We've prepared for Miami, for the Jets, for Baltimore, but we just haven't looked at them."

What everyone was looking at late in the second quarter was Bledsoe at quarterback. Brady hurt his left ankle when hit by safety Lee Flowers and limped to the sideline with 1:40 remaining in the half. On came Bledsoe for his first significant action since getting hurt in Game 2.

If there were any remaining questions about the Pats' destiny—a meeting with the powerhouse Rams in the Super Bowl—they should have been erased right there. Bledsoe guided his team 40 yards in four plays, with an 11-yard touchdown pass to Patten making it 14-3.

Special teams took over from there, with a blocked field goal and a punt returned for touchdowns in a 24-17 win.

"I've done this for a long time and at times at a pretty high level," Bledsoe said. "I felt confident coming out. I've been working hard and preparing for this exact scenario."

Hardly anyone outside of Foxboro had been prepared for this scenario: New England vs. St. Louis at the New Orleans Superdome in the 2002 Super Bowl.

"The only way we're going to get our respect is by winning the whole damn thing," Milloy insisted. "I've never heard of a lucky Super Bowl champion."

To win their first NFL championship—the Patriots lost in January 1986 to Chicago and 11 years later to Green Bay in their other visits to the big game—they would need to overcome the mighty Rams. Two years previously, St. Louis edged Tennessee to win the crown. The 2001 Rams squad was even more formidable and more experienced than that team.

St. Louis was installed as a 14-point favorite.

Questions about Brady's health and the Patriots' mind-set if Bledsoe started contributed to that big spread. So did the collection of stars in St. Louis, from league MVP Kurt Warner to Marshall Faulk to Isaac Bruce, Torry Holt, and Orlando Pace. And the first result between the teams, a 24-17 win for St. Louis in November that was New England's most recent defeat.

Mostly, there was the perception that the Patriots were in "Nawlins" on a fluke, that they'd used some kind of Bayou voodoo to get this far. Or some Salem witchcraft.

The Super Bowl setting was somewhat eerie, too. It was unlike any before it. Security was so strict that anyone without tickets couldn't get within two blocks of the Superdome. Those with tickets were subjected to lengthy and thorough searches of their property, as well as having to pass through metal detectors.

Everywhere outside the stadium, the enhanced protection was palpable. Inside the dome, there were enough police officers and plainclothes cops to safeguard dozens of presidents and prime ministers and chancellors.

"We will always be alert to the possibility of a terrorist event at a high-profile event like the Super Bowl, like the Olympics," Homeland Security director Tom Ridge said on NBC-TV's *Meet the Press*.

When the attention turned to football, the questions about Brady were answered early: He was healthy and would play.

As for slowing down the vaunted Rams scoring machine, did Belichick, the defensive mastermind, have any solutions?

"We're not going to be able to win this game offensively," Belichick said, stating the obvious—and nothing more.

But Belichick was ready. It was, after all, his brilliant schemes in the 1991 Super Bowl that helped the Giants slow down just as potent an attack on their way to upsetting Buffalo.

Against the Rams, Belichick told his defenders to be more

physical than ever. Make those tackles hurt. He emphasized that point particularly with his cornerbacks and safeties, and from the first play, they brutalized St. Louis's outstanding receivers.

Mostly, the Patriots put pressure on Warner. They blitzed linebackers and defensive backs. They mixed up their rushing patterns. They used different personnel packages than the Rams planned for.

Warner was hurried and harried—and hit—all game. His favorite weapon, deep passes, was taken away by the stingy, aggressive Pats.

"We never let him get comfortable," defensive lineman Richard Seymour said. "Anytime we can get him shifting out of his comfort zone—out of the pocket, moving around—that's to our advantage."

Law returned an interception for a touchdown, another pickoff led to a field goal, and the Patriots built a 17-3 lead. With less than 10 minutes remaining, this miracle season was about to conclude with the perfect ending for New England.

Desperate, the Rams made a last-ditch rally. Coach Mike Martz stubbornly had refused to run the ball, even though he had the superb Faulk in the backfield, and his strategy had backfired. Late in the game, though, he had no choice. St. Louis had to throw, had to rely on Warner, the NFL's most prolific passer, to carry it back.

Warner made a key adjustment by rolling out of the pocket on some passes. Hardly his strength in the past, it worked because it was unexpected. For all of Belichick's preparations, this was one thing he didn't prepare for—Warner scrambling around.

Warner led two late scoring drives. He scored himself on a 2-yard run to make it 17-10. The Rams' defense held, and St. Louis needed only 21 seconds to tie it, a 55-yard drive capped by a 26-yard pass from Warner to Ricky Proehl with 1:30 left.

Overtime, for the first time in Super Bowl history?

The Patriots had other ideas. Brady had other ideas. Brown had other ideas.

New England began its decisive drive from its 17-yard line with 1:21 left in the fourth quarter and with no timeouts. The Patriots never thought about running out the clock and taking their chances in an extra period, even though any sort of mistake could give the Rams an opportunity to win it before time expired.

"Our goal was to move the ball down the field to get into field-goal range," Brady said. "I was planning to go out there and win the game."

Brady already had achieved a memorable comeback victory in "the Tuck Game." So why not another?

He hit backup running back J. R. Redmond for 5 and 8 yards to the New England 30. After a spike, he again found Redmond at the 41. On second down, Brown got open across the middle for 26 yards before sprinting to the sideline and out of bounds to stop the clock.

With 21 seconds left, the Patriots were at the 36. Belichick never hesitated, ordering one more play to get Vinatieri closer. Brady didn't hesitate, either, passing to Wiggins for 6 yards. After the tackle, he hurried the Patriots to the line and spiked the ball with :07 on the clock.

Out trotted Vinatieri. And he was a bundle of nerves, right? Uh, no.

"I kicked that field goal 1,000 times in my sleep last night," he said. "It's kind of one of those things that us young kickers think about: making the kick to win the Super Bowl."

From 48 yards, Vinatieri's kick was true. Patriots 20, Rams 17.

"The Raider one was probably harder, but this one's a little bit more special," Vinatieri said. "Both kicks were pretty incredible."

*Adam Vinatieri punches the sky following his game-winning field goal with seven seconds left on the clock in the 2002 Super Bowl against the heavily favored St. Louis Rams.*

As were the past five months for this team, which entered the season as 50-1 long shots to win it all.

"There are so many variables, and you just need a few things to fall in place," Patriots director of player personnel Scott Pioli said. "I don't think teams go into the offseason saying, 'We can make the Super Bowl.' I think you go into it with the goal of improving, and then you see where you go from there."

Against heavy odds, the Patriots went as far as you can.